A FEAST FOR THE SOUL

Meditations on the Attributes of God and of Humanity

A Compilation

Other Books in the Bahá'í Holy Day Series

The Passing of 'Abdu'l-Bahá: A Compilation
The Ascension of Bahá'u'lláh: A Compilation
Days of Ridván: A Compilation
Naw-Rúz—New Day: A Compilation
Twin Holy Days: A Compilation
Martyrdom of the Báb: A Compilation
Declaration of the Báb: A Compilation

Bahá'í Prayerbook Series

Bahá'í Prayers for Women
Healing the Soul: Prayers of Comfort & Renewal
Prayers of Ecstasy
Spiritual Strength for Men

A FEAST FOR THE SOUL

Meditations on the Attributes of God and of Humanity

A Compilation

Selections from the Writings of Bahá'u'lláh,
the Báb, 'Abdu'l-Bahá, and the Greatest Holy Leaf

KALIMÁT PRESS
LOS ANGELES

Library of Congress Cataloging-in-Publication Data

A feast for the soul : meditations on the attributes of God :
   selections from the writings of Bahá'u'lláh, the Báb,
   'Abdu'l-Bahá, and the Greatest Holy Leaf : a compilation.
      p. cm. -- (Baha'i holy days)
   Includes bibliographical references and index.
   ISBN 1-890688-43-6 (hard cover : alk. paper)
   1. God--Attributes--Meditations. 2. Bahai meditations. 3.
Bahai Faith--Quotations, maxims, etc. I. Bahá'u'lláh, 1817-
1892. II. Series.
BP360.F43 2006
297.9'32112--dc22

                                        2005031569

Kalimát Press
1600 Sawtelle Boulevard
Suite 310
Los Angeles, California 90025

orders@kalimat.com
www.kalimat.com

CONTENTS

months
of the Bahá'í calendar

1st	Bahá	Splendor	March 21
2nd	Jalál	Glory	April 9
3rd	Jamál	Beauty	April 28
4th	'Azamat	Grandeur	May 17
5th	Núr	Light	June 5
6th	Rahmat	Mercy	June 24
7th	Kalimát	Words	July 13
8th	Kamál	Perfection	August 1
9th	Asmá'	Names	August 20
10th	'Izzat	Might	September 8
11th	Mashíyyat	Will	September 27
12th	'Ilm	Knowledge	October 16
13th	Qudrat	Power	November 4
14th	Qawl	Speech	November 23
15th	Masá'il	Questions	December 12
16th	Sharaf	Honor	December 31
17th	Sultán	Sovereignty	January 19
18th	Mulk	Dominion	February 7
19th	'Alá'	Loftiness	March 2

PREFACE

IN ISLAMIC TRADITION, although not all of the names of God are known, there are ninety-nine names of God that can be listed. These names all refer to God's attributes—the Compassionate, the Merciful, the Holy, the Preserver, the Generous, the Protector, the Hidden, the Self-Subsisting, and so forth. And, all of the names of God are considered beautiful. The Qur'an says—"*The most beautiful Names belong to God, so call on Him by them* . . .[1]

There are various lists of the ninety-nine names, and they do not always agree. Despite the variations, Muslims regard it as an act of piety to recite the list of God's names. Some just do this by rote. Others believe that it is their duty, not just to speak the names, but to emulate these attributes in their lives.

Tradition also recounts that there is one more name, the one-hundredth name, which is hidden, but is regarded—especially by the Sufis—as the Greatest Name of God. Some of the prophecies in Islamic tradition suggest that this name will be revealed only by the

Promised One (the Qá'im or the Mahdí) on the Day of
Judgment. For Bahá'ís, this Greatest Name is the name
of Bahá'u'lláh. Any form of the name *Bahá* (light, glory,
splendor) or *Abhá* (the superlative form, most glorious)
—or any invocation of that name, such as *Yá Bahá'u'l-
Abhá!* (O Thou Glory of the All-Glorious!) or *Alláh-u
Abhá* (God is Most Glorious)—is considered the
Greatest Name.

THE BAHÁ'Í TEACHINGS insist that God is infinite and
unknowable, and therefore forever beyond human
understanding or imagination. Strictly speaking, then,
God has no attributes or names. In the Long Obligatory
Prayer, Bahá'u'lláh reveals this verse, addressing God:
*"Too high art Thou for the praise of those who are nigh unto
Thee to ascend unto the heaven of Thy nearness, or for the
birds of the hearts of them who are devoted to Thee to attain
to the door of Thy gate. I testify that Thou hast been sanctified above all attributes and holy above all names."*

Nonetheless, praise and magnification of the names
of God are found everywhere in the Bahá'í sacred scriptures—particularly in the writings of Bahá'u'lláh. In fact,
the next sentence in the Obligatory Prayer reads: *"No
God is there but Thee, the Most Exalted, the All-Glorious."*
These names have important and multiple meanings in
Bahá'í scriptures.

First of all, although all of the names are addressed
to God, they also refer to the qualities and attributes of
the Manifestations of God. These qualities are human

characteristics, of course, and so cannot refer to God's essence. But these attributes are demonstrated to perfection by God's prophets. 'Abdu'l-Bahá has explained:

> All the perfections, the bounties, the splendors which come from God are visible and evident in the Reality of the Holy Manifestations . . . all the praises, the descriptions and exaltations refer to the Holy Manifestations—that is to say, all the descriptions, the qualities, the names and the attributes which we mention [in praise of God] return to the Divine Manifestations; but as no one has attained to the reality of the Essence of Divinity, so no one is able to describe, explain, praise or glorify it. Therefore, all that the human reality knows, discovers and understands of the names, the attributes and the perfections of God refer to these Holy Manifestations. There is no access to anything else: "the way is closed, and seeking is forbidden."[2]

Therefore, for Bahá'ís, the names of God actually refer to the qualities of the Manifestations of God. But beyond that, these are qualities that all human beings potentially share and must strive to embody. Since we are unable to praise God with his own perfections, because they are infinitely beyond human comprehension, we must praise him with the highest human aspirations—love, justice, mercy, compassion, generosity, wisdom, pity, and so forth. In this way, we remind ourselves of the highest and best of what we can achieve. Bahá'u'lláh makes this explicit. Addressing God, he affirms:

> Far, far from Thy glory be what mortal man can affirm of Thee, or attribute unto Thee, or the praise with which he can glorify Thee! Whatever duty Thou hast prescribed

unto Thy servants of extolling to the utmost Thy majesty
and glory is but a token of Thy grace unto them, that they
may be enabled to ascend unto the station conferred upon
their own inmost being, the station of the knowledge of
their own selves.[3]

By praising God we are taught to recognize our own spiritual potential and to honor our own higher selves. The
attributes of God are, in reality, the highest attributes of
humankind.

THE BAHÁ'Í CALENDAR was inaugurated by the Báb and
adopted by Bahá'u'lláh as the religious calendar for this
dispensation. It consists of nineteen months, each of
which has nineteen days, and four or five intercalary
days that fall before the beginning of the last month of
the year. Each of the nineteen months is given one of
the names of God. The days of each month are also
named, and the names of the days of the month are the
same as the names of the months of the year. The first
day of each month is thus the day of Bahá (Splendor)
and the last day of each month is the day of 'Alá'
(Loftiness).

The names of the days and the months were clearly
gleaned by the Báb from Islamic tradition for use in his
calendar. The Research Department of the Universal
House of Justice has provided this clarification of the
sources of these names:

A study of the Writings of the Báb shows that the names of God have been revealed in His Scriptures repeatedly and in different ways, and the most common of those names are those closely related to the [Islamic] Ramadan "Dawn Prayers." The names of the months of the Bayán are generally the same as in the said prayers, and . . . Nabíl-i Zarandí has given the source of his quotation of the names as the Kitáb-i Asmá' . . . [4]

Meanwhile, the names of all the months of the Bayán have not been given clearly, but since in the Book of Bayán the name of the first month is given as Bahá and the last month as 'Alá' (Persian Bayán, Unit 5, Chapter 3), Nabíl may have taken the names of the months from one of the Writings of the Báb revealed on the basis of the "Dawn Prayers."[5]

In one remarkable passage, the Báb writes in praise of Him Whom God shall make manifest (i.e., Bahá'-u'lláh) using most of the names of the months of the year:

> The *glory* of Him Whom God shall make manifest is immeasurably above every other glory, and His majesty is far above every other majesty. His *beauty* excelleth every other embodiment of beauty, and His *grandeur* immensely exceedeth every other manifestation of grandeur. Every *light* paleth before the radiance of His light, and every other exponent of *mercy* falleth short before the tokens of His mercy. Every other *perfection* is as naught in the face of His consummate perfection, and every other display of *might* is as nothing before His absolute might. His *names* are superior to all other names. His good-pleasure taketh precedence over any other expression of good-pleasure. His pre-eminent exaltation is far above the reach of every other

symbol of exaltation. The *splendor* of His appearance far surpasseth that of any other appearance. His divine concealment is far more profound than any other concealment. His *loftiness* is immeasurably above every other loftiness. His gracious favor is unequalled by any other evidence of favor. His *power* transcendeth every power. His *sovereignty* is invincible in the face of every other sovereignty. His celestial *dominion* is exalted far above every other dominion. His *knowledge* pervadeth all created things, and His consummate power extendeth over all beings.[6]

IN THIS COMPILATION, there are collected together quotations from the Bahá'í sacred writings on themes that are suggested by the names of the months of the Bahá'í calendar. The compilation is by no means exhaustive: there are any number of additional passages to be found in the writings on these names and attributes of God and of humanity. These passages are simply a selection made, more or less arbitrarily, by the compilers.

It has become customary in many Bahá'í communities to choose readings for the Nineteen-Day Feasts based on the names of the Bahá'í months. So, the devotional readings at the Feast of Kalimát might be focused on the "Words" of God, for example; and the readings at the Feast of Qudrat might be concerned with God's "Power." This is not required, of course, and any passages from the sacred writings are appropriately read at any Feast, regardless of its name. Therefore, the chapters of this book are not intended for use as Feast programs, per se. It is not the intention of the editors that any rigid practice should develop around this compilation or that any of the passages that have been selected should become identified exclusively with any one Feast. Certainly, it would be neither desirable nor appropriate to publish a fixed set of readings for the Nineteen-Day Feast that would be used ritualistically or unthinkingly every month.

However, we are hopeful that this compilation will be useful to Bahá'í communities as they seek to put together their own unique programs for their observances of the Nineteen-Day Feasts. In addition, the book may have other uses, as well. We hope that it will be used as a sourcebook for personal reflection, meditation, and study. Since nineteen quotations are provided for each Bahá'í month, it can be used as a book of daily readings and a reference for the Bahá'í calendar. Naturally, beyond this, the Bahá'í scriptures have endless uses and are always a fresh source of comfort and inspiration for the believers.

THE EDITORS

NOTES

1. Qur'an 7:180.
2. 'Abdu'l-Bahá, *Some Answered Questions*, pp. 147-48.
3. Bahá'u'lláh, *Gleanings*, pp. 4-5.
4. See Nabíl's explanation of the Badí' calendar in various volumes of *The Bahá'í World*, in the article entitled "Additional Material Gleaned from Nabíl's Narrative (Vol. II), regarding the Bahá'í Calendar."

5. Research Department to the Universal House of Justice, quoted in *Selected Readings for 19-Day Feasts classified according to the names of Bahá'í months in the Badí' calendar*, by Elias Zohoori (Jamaica: by the author, 2001), pp. iv-v.
6. The Báb, *Selections*, pp. 156-67. (Emphasis added.)

A FEAST FOR THE SOUL

Meditations on the Attributes of God and of Humanity

A Compilation

SPLENDOR

Bahá

This is the Day whereon naught can be seen except the splendors of the Light that shineth from the face of Thy Lord, the Gracious, the Most Bountiful.

—Bahá'u'lláh

March 21

1 The Eternal Truth is now come. He hath lifted up the Ensign of Power, and is now shedding upon the world the unclouded splendor of His Revelation.

—Bahá'u'lláh

March 22

2 See ye not this Sun that shineth in refulgent splendor above the All-Glorious Horizon?

—Bahá'u'lláh

March 23

3 Verily, all created things were immersed in the sea of purification when, on that first day of Riḍván, We shed upon the whole of creation the splendors of Our

3

most excellent Names and Our most exalted Attributes. This, verily, is a token of My loving providence, which hath encompassed all the worlds.

—Bahá'u'lláh

March 24

4 He that was hidden from mortal eyes is come! His all-conquering sovereignty is manifest; His all-encompassing splendor is revealed.

—Bahá'u'lláh

march 25

5 Happy the one who entereth upon the first day of the month of Bahá, the day which God hath consecrated to this Great Name. And blessed be he who evidenceth on this day the bounties that God hath bestowed upon him; he, verily, is of those who show forth thanks to God through actions betokening the Lord's munificence which hath encompassed all the worlds.

Say: This day, verily, is the crown of all the months and the source thereof, the day on which the breath of life is wafted over all created things. Great is the blessedness of him who greeteth it with radiance and joy. We testify that he is, in truth, among those who are blissful.

—Bahá'u'lláh

march 26

6 Our mission is to seize and possess the hearts of men. Upon them the eyes of Bahá are fastened.

—Bahá'u'lláh

7 Every receptive soul who hath in this Day inhaled the fragrance of His garment and hath, with a pure heart, set his face towards the all-glorious Horizon is reckoned among the people of Bahá in the Crimson Book.

Grasp ye, in My Name, the chalice of My loving-kindness, drink then your fill in My glorious and wondrous remembrance.

—Bahá'u'lláh

March 28

8 Blessed are the people of Bahá! God beareth Me witness! They are the solace of the eye of creation. Through them the universes have been adorned, and the Preserved Tablet embellished. They are the ones who have sailed on the <u>ark of complete independence</u>, with their faces set towards the Dayspring of Beauty. How great is their blessedness that they have attained unto what their Lord, the Omniscient, the All-Wise, hath willed. Through their light the heavens have been adorned, and the faces of those that have drawn nigh unto Him made to shine.

—Bahá'u'lláh

March 29

9 The people of Bahá. Through them have been shed the splendors of the light of guidance.

—Bahá'u'lláh

March 30

10 O people of Bahá! Ye are the breezes of spring that are wafted over the world. Through you We have adorned the world of being with the ornament of the knowledge of the Most Merciful. Through you the countenance of the world hath been wreathed in smiles, and the brightness of His light shone forth. Cling ye to the Cord of steadfastness, in such wise that all vain imaginings may utterly vanish.

—Bahá'u'lláh

March 21

11 O my God, Thou hast enabled me to know Thee, and through the radiance of Thine effulgent splendor Thou hast inspired me with Thy remembrance.

—The Báb

April 1

12 I beseech Thee, O my Lord, by Thy most effulgent splendor, before whose brightness every soul humbly boweth down and prostrateth itself in adoration for Thy sake—a splendor before whose radiance fire is turned into light, the dead are brought to life and every difficulty is changed into ease.

I entreat Thee by this great, this wondrous splendor and by the glory of Thine exalted sovereignty, O Thou Who art the Lord of indomitable power, to transform us through Thy bounty into that which Thou Thyself dost possess and enable us to become fountains of Thy light, and graciously vouchsafe unto us that which beseemeth the majesty of Thy transcendent dominion.

For unto Thee have I raised my hands, O Lord, and in Thee have I found sheltering support, O Lord, and unto Thee have I resigned myself, O Lord, and upon Thee have I placed my whole reliance, O Lord, and by Thee am I strengthened, O Lord.

Verily there is no power nor strength except in Thee.

—The Báb

April 2

13 O ye illumined loved ones and ye handmaids of the Merciful!

At a time when the somber night of ignorance, of neglect of the divine world, of being veiled from God, had overspread the earth, a bright morning dawned and a rising light lit up the eastern sky. Then rose the Sun of Truth and the splendors of the Kingdom were shed over east and west. Those who had eyes to see rejoiced at the glad tidings and cried out: "O blessed, blessed are we!" . . .

—'Abdu'l-Bahá

April 3

14 O God, my God! I beg of Thee by the dawning of the light of Thy Beauty that hath illumined all the earth, and by the glance of Thy divine compassion's eye that considereth all things, and by the surging sea of Thy bestowals in which all things are immersed, and by Thy streaming clouds of bounty raining down gifts upon the essences of all created things, and by the splendors of Thy mercy that existed before ever the world was—to help Thy chosen ones to be faithful, and assist Thy loved ones to serve at Thine exalted Threshold, and cause them to gain the victory through the battalions of Thy might that overpowereth all things, and reinforce them with a great fighting host from out of the Concourse on high.

—'Abdu'l-Bahá

15 Grant, O Thou Loving Lord, that all may stand firm and steadfast, shining with everlasting splendor, so that, at every breath, gentle breezes may blow from the bowers of Thy loving-kindness, that from the ocean of Thy grace a mist may rise, that the kindly showers of Thy love may bestow freshness, and the zephyr waft its perfume from the rose garden of divine unity.

—'Abdu'l-Bahá

16 Praise thou God that thou hast found thy way into the Kingdom of Splendors, and hast rent asunder the veil of vain imaginings, and that the core of the inner mystery hath been made known unto thee.

—'Abdu'l-Bahá

17 The Cause of God is spreading, and manifest in splendor are the wonders from on high. The east is illumined and the west perfumed; fragrant with ambergris is the north, and musk-scented the south.

—'Abdu'l-Bahá

18 Serve ye the Cause of God. Face ye all nations of the world with the constancy and the endurance of the people of Bahá, that all men may be astounded and ask how this could be, that your hearts are as well-springs of confidence and faith, and as mines so rich in the love of God.

—'Abdu'l-Bahá

19 O thou seeker after truth!
The world of the Kingdom is one world. The only difference is that spring returneth over and over again, and setteth up a great new commotion throughout all created things. Then plain and hillside come alive, and trees turn delicately green, and leaves, blossoms and fruits come forth in beauty, infinite and tender. Wherefore the dispensations of past ages are intimately connected with those that follow them: indeed, they are one and the same, but as the world groweth, so doth the light, so doth the downpour of heavenly grace, and then the Day-Star shineth out in noonday splendor.

—'Abdu'l-Bahá

Praise be to Him through Whose splendors the earth and the heavens are aglow, through Whose fragrant breathings the gardens of holiness that adorn the hearts of the chosen

are trembling for joy, to Him Who hath shed His light and brightened the face of the firmament. Verily there appeared luminous and sparkling stars, glittering, shining out, and casting forth their rays upon the supreme horizon. They derived their grace and brilliance from the bounties of the Abhá Realm, then, stars of guidance, they poured down their lights upon this earth.

Praise be to Him Who hath fashioned this new era, this age of majesty, even as an unfolding pageant where the realities of all things can be exposed to view. Now are clouds of bounty raining down and the gifts of the loving Lord are clearly manifest; for both the seen and the unseen worlds have been illumined, and the Promised One hath come to earth and the beauty of the Adored One hath shone forth.

Salutations, blessings, and welcome to that Universal Reality, that Perfect Word, that Manifest Book, that Splendor which hath dawned in the highest heaven, that Guide of all nations, that Light of the world—the billowing ocean of Whose abounding grace hath flooded all creation, in such wise that the waves thereof have cast upon the sands of this visible world their shining pearls.

Now hath the Truth appeared, and falsehood fled away; now hath the day dawned and jubilation taken over, wherefore men's souls are sanctified, their spirits purged, their hearts rejoiced, their minds purified, their secret thoughts made wholesome, their consciences washed clean, their inmost selves made holy: for the Day of Resurrection hath come to pass, and the bestowals of thy Lord, the Forgiving, *have encompassed all things. Salutations and praise be unto those luminous, resplendent stars that are shedding down their rays from the highest heaven, those celestial bodies of the girdling zodiac of the Abhá Realm.*

May glory rest upon them.

—'Abdu'l-Bahá

GLORY

Jalál

*The whole earth is illuminated with the resplendent glory
of God's Revelation.*
—Bahá'u'lláh

1 He Who is the King of Kings hath appeared, arrayed
in His most wondrous glory . . .
—Bahá'u'lláh

2 All praise and glory be to Thee, Thou of Whom all
things have testified that Thou art one and there is
none other God but Thee, Who hast been from everlasting exalted above all peer or likeness and to everlasting shalt remain the same. All kings are but Thy servants
and all beings, visible and invisible, as naught before
Thee. There is none other God but Thee, the Gracious,
the Powerful, the Most High.
—Bahá'u'lláh

3 Glorified, immensely glorified art Thou! Thou art He Who from everlasting hath been the King of the entire creation and its Prime Mover, and Thou wilt to everlasting remain the Lord of all created things and their Ordainer.

Glorified art Thou, O my God! If Thou ceasest to be merciful unto Thy servants, who, then, will show mercy unto them; and if Thou refusest to succor Thy loved ones, who is there that can succor them?

Glorified, immeasurably glorified art Thou! Thou art adored in Thy truth, and Thee do we all, verily, worship; and Thou art manifest in Thy justice, and to Thee do we all, verily, bear witness. Thou art, in truth, beloved in Thy grace. No God is there but Thee, the Help in Peril, the Self-Subsisting.

—Bahá'u'lláh

4 All praise be to the one true God—exalted be His glory—inasmuch as He hath, through the Pen of the Most High, unlocked the doors of men's hearts. Every verse which this Pen hath revealed is a bright and shining portal that discloseth the glories of a saintly and pious life, of pure and stainless deeds.

—Bahá'u'lláh

5 Exalted, immeasurably exalted, is His detachment above the reach and ken of the entire creation! Glorified, glorified be His meekness—a meekness that

hath melted the hearts of them that have been brought nigh unto God!

—Bahá'u'lláh

6 My glory be with thee and with those of My loved ones that associate with thee. These indeed are they with whom it shall be well.

—Bahá'u'lláh

7 O Son of Glory!
Be swift in the path of holiness, and enter the heaven of communion with Me.

—Bahá'u'lláh

8 All that is in heaven and earth I have ordained for thee, except the human heart, which I have made the habitation of My beauty and glory . . .

—Bahá'u'lláh

9 O Son of Being!
If poverty overtake thee, be not sad; for in time the Lord of wealth shall visit thee. Fear not abasement, for glory shall one day rest on thee.

—Bahá'u'lláh

10 O My servants! Sorrow not if, in these days and on this earthly plane, things contrary to your wishes have been ordained and manifested by God, for days of blissful joy, of heavenly delight, are assuredly in store for ✳

you. Worlds, holy and spiritually glorious, will be unveiled to your eyes. You are destined by Him, in this world and hereafter, to partake of their benefits, to share in their joys, and to obtain a portion of their sustaining grace. To each and every one of them you will, no doubt, attain.

—Bahá'u'lláh

11 Glory be to Thee, O God!
Thou art the God Who hath existed before all things, Who will exist after all things and will last beyond all things. Thou art the God Who knoweth all things, and is supreme over all things. Thou art the God Who dealeth mercifully with all things, Who judgeth between all things and Whose vision embraceth all things.

—The Báb

12 There is one God; mankind is one; the foundations of religion are one. Let us worship Him, and give praise for all His great Prophets and Messengers who have manifested His brightness and glory.

—'Abdu'l-Bahá

13 This will be the paradise which is to come on earth, when all mankind will be gathered together under the tent of unity in the Kingdom of Glory.

—'Abdu'l-Bahá

14 Bahá'u'lláh has risen from the eastern horizon. Like the glory of the sun He has come into the world. He has reflected the reality of divine religion, dispelled the darkness of imitations, laid the foundation of new teachings and resuscitated the world.

—'Abdu'l-Bahá

15 O ye beloved, and ye handmaids of the Merciful! This is the day when the Day-Star of Truth rose over the horizon of life, and its glory spread, and its brightness shone out with such power that it clove the dense and high-piled clouds and mounted the skies of the world in all its splendor.

—'Abdu'l-Bahá

16 No stir is there in the world save that of the Glory of the One Ravisher of Hearts, and no tumult is there save the surging of the love of Him, the Incomparable, the Well-Beloved.

—'Abdu'l-Bahá

17 The noblest of men is he who serves humankind, and he is nearest the threshold of God who is the least of His servants. The glory and majesty of man are dependent upon his servitude to his fellow creatures . . .

—'Abdu'l-Bahá

18 Erelong shall your faces be bright with the radiance of your supplications and your worship of God, your prayers unto Him, and your humility and selflessness in the presence of the friends. He will make of your assemblage a magnet that will draw unto you the bright rays of divine confirmations that shine out from His kingdom of glory.

—'Abdu'l-Bahá

19 Remove not, O Lord, the festal board that hath been spread in Thy Name, and extinguish not the burning flame that hath been kindled by Thine unquenchable fire. Withhold not from flowing that living water of Thine that murmureth with the melody of Thy glory and Thy remembrance, and deprive not Thy servants from the fragrance of Thy sweet savors breathing forth the perfume of Thy love.

Lord! Turn the distressing cares of Thy holy ones into ease, their hardship into comfort, their abasement into glory, their sorrow into blissful joy, O Thou that holdest in Thy grasp the reins of all mankind!

Thou art, verily, the One, the Single, the Mighty, the All-Knowing, the All-Wise.

—'Abdu'l-Bahá

Glory be to Thee, O my God!
  Behold me, then, O my God, *fallen prostrate upon the dust before Thee, confessing my powerlessness and Thine*

omnipotence, my poverty and Thy wealth, mine evanescence and Thine eternity, mine utter abasement and Thine infinite glory. I recognize that there is none other God but Thee, that Thou hast no peer nor partner, none to equal or rival Thee. In Thine unapproachable loftiness Thou hast, from eternity, been exalted above the praise of any one but Thee, and shalt continue for ever, in Thy transcendent singleness and glory, to be sanctified from the glorification of any one except Thine own Self. . . . Glorified, glorified be Thine unattainable loftiness. Glorified, glorified be the preeminence of Thy kingship and the sublimity of Thine authority and power.

Glorified, glorified be Thou, O my God! How can I ever hope to ascend into the heaven of Thy most holy will, or gain admittance into the tabernacle of Thy Divine knowledge, knowing as I do that the minds of the wise and learned are impotent to fathom the secrets of Thy handiwork—a handiwork which is itself but a creation of Thy will?

Praise be to Thee, O Lord, my God, my Master, my Possessor, my King. Now that I have confessed unto Thee my powerlessness and the powerlessness of all created things, and have acknowledged my poverty and the poverty of the entire creation, I call unto Thee with my tongue and the tongues of all that are in heaven and on earth, and beseech Thee with my heart and the hearts of all that have entered beneath the shadow of Thy names and Thine attributes, not to shut us from the doors of Thy loving-kindness and grace, nor to suffer the breeze of Thy bountiful care and favor to cease from being wafted over our souls, nor to permit that our hearts be occupied with any one except Thee, or our minds to be busied with any remembrance save remembrance of Thy Self.

By the glory of Thy might, O my God! Wert Thou to set me king over Thy realms, and to establish me upon the throne of Thy sovereignty, and to deliver, through Thy power, the reins of the entire creation into my hands, and wert Thou to cause me, though it be for less than a moment, to be occupied with these things and be oblivious of the wondrous memories associated with Thy most mighty, most perfect, and most exalted Name, my soul would still remain unsatisfied, and the pangs of my heart unstilled. Nay, I would, in that very state, recognize myself as the poorest of the poor, and the most wretched of the wretched.

Magnified be Thy name, O my God! Now that Thou hast caused me to apprehend this truth, I beseech Thee by Thy Name which no scroll can bear, which no heart can imagine and no tongue can utter—a Name which will remain concealed so long as Thine own Essence is hidden, and will be glorified so long as Thine own Being is extolled—to unfurl, ere the present year draw to a close, the ensigns of Thine undisputed ascendancy and triumph, that the whole creation may be enriched by Thy wealth, and may be exalted through the ennobling influence of Thy transcendent sovereignty, and that all may arise and promote Thy Cause.

—Bahá'u'lláh

Beauty

Jamál

*. . . that which eternally endureth is the Beauty of
the True One . . .*
—'Abdu'l-Bahá

1 Rejoice in the gladness of thine heart, that thou
mayest be worthy to meet Me and to mirror forth My
beauty.

—Bahá'u'lláh

2 O Friends! Abandon not the everlasting beauty for
a beauty that must die, and set not your affections
on this mortal world of dust.

—Bahá'u'lláh

3 O Fleeting Shadow!
Pass beyond the baser stages of doubt and rise to
the exalted heights of certainty. Open the eye of truth,

that thou mayest behold the veilless Beauty and exclaim:
Hallowed be the Lord, the most excellent of all creators!

—Bahá'u'lláh

4 Lo, the Nightingale of Paradise singeth upon the
twigs of the Tree of Eternity, with holy and sweet
melodies, proclaiming to the sincere ones the glad tidings of the nearness of God, calling the believers in the
Divine Unity to the court of the Presence of the
Generous One, informing the severed ones of the mes-
sage which hath been revealed by God, the King, the
Glorious, the Peerless, guiding the lovers to the seat of
sanctity and to this resplendent Beauty.

Verily this is that Most Great Beauty, foretold in the
Books of the Messengers, through Whom truth shall be
distinguished from error and the wisdom of every command shall be tested. Verily He is the Tree of Life that
bringeth forth the fruits of God, the Exalted, the
Powerful, the Great.

—Bahá'u'lláh

5 . . . enrich Thyself increasingly, in the kingdom of
creation, with the incorruptible vestures of Thy
God, that the beauteous image of the Almighty may be
reflected through Thee in all created things . . .

—Bahá'u'lláh

6 I beseech Thee, O my God, by Thy Beauty that shineth forth above the horizon of eternity, a Beauty before which as soon as it revealeth itself the kingdom of beauty boweth down in worship, magnifying it in ringing tones, to grant that I may die to all that I possess and live to whatsoever belongeth unto Thee.

—Bahá'u'lláh

7 O my Lord! Make Thy beauty to be my food, and Thy presence my drink, and Thy pleasure my hope, and praise of Thee my action, and remembrance of Thee my companion, and the power of Thy sovereignty my succorer, and Thy habitation my home, and my dwelling-place the seat Thou hast sanctified from the limitations imposed upon them who are shut out as by a veil from Thee.

Thou art, verily, the Almighty, the All-Glorious, the Most Powerful.

—Bahá'u'lláh

8 Make me ready, in all circumstances, O my Lord, to serve Thee and to set myself towards the adored sanctuary of Thy Revelation and of Thy Beauty.

If it be Thy pleasure, make me to grow as a tender herb in the meadows of Thy grace, that the gentle winds of Thy will may stir me up and bend me into conformity with Thy pleasure, in such wise that my movement and my stillness may be wholly directed by Thee.

—Bahá'u'lláh

9 Be Thou, O my Lord, my sole Desire, my Goal, mine only Hope, my constant Aim, my Habitation and my Sanctuary. Let the object of mine ardent quest be Thy most resplendent, Thine adorable, and ever-blessed Beauty. I implore Thee, O my Lord, by whatsoever is of Thee, to send, from the right hand of Thy might, that which will exalt Thy loved ones and abase Thine enemies.

No God is there beside Thee, Thou alone art my Beloved in this world and in the world which is to come. Thou alone art the Desire of all them that have recognized Thee.

Praised be God, the Lord of the worlds.

—Bahá'u'lláh

10 His beauty excelleth every other embodiment of beauty, and His grandeur immensely exceedeth every other manifestation of grandeur.

—The Báb

11 Number me, O my God, with those who are privileged to fix their gaze upon Thy Beauty and who take such delight therein that they would not exchange a single moment thereof with the sovereignty of the kingdom of heavens and earth or with the entire realm of creation.

—The Báb

12 O my Lord, my Beloved, my Desire!
Befriend me in my loneliness and accompany me in my exile. Remove my sorrow. Cause me to be devoted to Thy beauty.

—'Abdu'l-Bahá

13 O ye loved ones of God!
Loose your tongues and offer Him thanks; praise ye and glorify the Beauty of the Adored One, for ye have drunk from this purest of chalices, and ye are cheered and set aglow with this wine. Ye have detected the sweet scents of holiness, ye have smelled the musk of faithfulness from Joseph's raiment. Ye have fed on the honeydew of loyalty from the hands of Him Who is the one alone Beloved, ye have feasted on immortal dishes at the bounteous banquet table of the Lord.

—'Abdu'l-Bahá

14 O Thou loving Provider!
These souls have hearkened to the summons of the Kingdom, and have gazed upon the glory of the Sun of Truth. They have risen upward to the refreshing skies of love; they are enamored of Thy nature, and they worship Thy beauty. Unto Thee have they turned themselves, speaking together of Thee, seeking out Thy dwelling, and thirsting for the waterbrooks of Thy heavenly realm.

Thou art the Giver, the Bestower, the Ever-loving.

—'Abdu'l-Bahá

15 O holy Lord! O Lord of loving-kindness!
We stray about Thy dwelling, longing to behold Thy beauty, and loving all Thy ways. We are hapless, lowly, and of small account. We are paupers: show us mercy, give us bounty; look not upon our failings, hide Thou our endless sins. Whatever we are, still are we Thine, and what we speak and hear is praise of Thee, and it is Thy face we seek, Thy path we follow. Thou art the Lord of loving-kindness . . .

—'Abdu'l-Bahá

16 The love which exists between the hearts of believers is prompted by the ideal of the unity of spirits. This love is attained through the knowledge of God, so that men see the Divine Love reflected in the heart. Each sees in the other the Beauty of God reflected in the soul, and finding this point of similarity, they are attracted to one another in love.

—'Abdu'l-Bahá

17 Praised be Thou, O my Lord!
Thou hast guided the distracted out of the death of unbelief, and hast brought those who draw nigh unto Thee to the journey's goal, and hast rejoiced the assured among Thy servants by granting them their most cherished desires, and hast, from Thy Kingdom of beauty, opened before the faces of those who yearn after Thee the gates of reunion, and hast rescued them from the fires of deprivation and loss—so that they hastened

unto Thee and gained Thy presence, and arrived at Thy welcoming door, and received of gifts an abundant share.

—'Abdu'l-Bahá

18 O ye loved ones of God!
The Sun of Truth is shining down from invisible skies; know ye the value of these days. Lift up your heads, and grow ye cypress-tall in these swift-running streams. Take ye joy in the beauty of the narcissus of Najd, for night will fall and it will be no more.

—'Abdu'l-Bahá

19 I leave you with a prayer that all the beauty of the Kingdom may be yours.

—'Abdu'l-Bahá

Behold me, then, O my God, how I have fled from myself unto Thee, and have abandoned my own being that I may attain unto the splendors of the light of Thy Being, and have forsaken all that keepeth me back from Thee, and maketh me forgetful of Thee, in order that I may inhale the fragrances of Thy presence and Thy remembrance. Behold how I have stepped upon the dust of the city of Thy forgiveness and Thy bounty, and dwelt within the precincts of Thy

transcendent mercy, and have besought Thee, through the sovereignty of Him Who is Thy Remembrance and Who hath appeared in the robe of Thy most pure and most august Beauty, to send down, in the course of this year, upon Thy loved ones what will enable them to dispense with any one except Thee, and will set them free to recognize the evidences of Thy sovereign will and all-conquering purpose, in such wise that they will seek only what Thou didst wish for them through Thy bidding, and will desire naught except what Thou didst desire for them through Thy will.

Sanctify, then, their eyes, O my God, that they may behold the light of Thy Beauty, and purge their ears, that they may listen to the melodies of the Dove of Thy transcendent oneness. Flood, then, their hearts with the wonders of Thy love, and preserve their tongues from mentioning any one save Thee, and guard their faces from turning to aught else except Thyself. Potent art Thou to do what pleaseth Thee. Thou, verily, art the Almighty, the Help in Peril, the Self-Subsisting.

Protect, moreover, O my Beloved, through Thy love for them and through the love they bear to Thee, this servant, who hath sacrificed his all for Thee, and expended whatsoever Thou hast given him in the path of Thy love and Thy good pleasure, and preserve him from all that Thou abhorrest, and from whatsoever may hinder him from entering into the Tabernacle of Thy holy sovereignty, and from attaining the seat of Thy transcendent oneness.

Number him, then, O my God, with such as have allowed nothing whatever to deter them from beholding Thy beauty, or from meditating on the wondrous evidences of Thine everlasting handiwork, that he may have fellowship with none except Thee, and turn to naught save Thyself, and discover in whatever hath been created by Thee in the kingdoms of earth and heaven nothing but Thy wondrous Beauty and the revelation of the splendors of Thy face, and be so immersed beneath the billowing oceans of Thine overruling providence and the surging seas of Thy holy unity, that he will forget every mention except the mention of Thy transcendent oneness, and banish from his soul the traces of all evil suggestions, O Thou in Whose hands are the kingdoms of all names and attributes!

—Bahá'u'lláh

GRANDEUR

※

'Azamat

*My majesty is My gift to thee, and My grandeur the token of
My mercy unto thee.*
—Bahá'u'lláh

1 How great is Thy power! How exalted Thy sovereignty! How lofty Thy might! How excellent Thy majesty! How supreme is Thy grandeur—a grandeur which He Who is Thy Manifestation hath made known . . .
—Bahá'u'lláh

2 The praise which hath dawned from Thy most august Self, and the glory which hath shone forth from Thy most effulgent Beauty, rest upon Thee, O Thou Who art the Manifestation of Grandeur, and the King of Eternity, and the Lord of all who are in heaven and on earth! I testify that through Thee the sovereignty of God and His dominion, and the majesty of God and

His grandeur, were revealed, and the Day-Stars of ancient splendor have shed their radiance in the heaven of Thine irrevocable decree, and the Beauty of the Unseen hath shone forth above the horizon of creation.

—Bahá'u'lláh

3 High, immeasurably high art Thou above the endeavors of the evanescent creature to soar unto the throne of Thine eternity, or of the poor and wretched to attain the summit of Thine all-sufficing glory! From eternity Thou didst Thyself describe Thine own Self unto Thy Self, and extol, in Thine own Essence, Thine Essence unto Thine Essence.

I swear by Thy glory, O my Best-Beloved! Who is there besides Thee that can claim to know Thee, and who save Thyself can make fitting mention of Thee? Thou art He Who, from eternity, abode in His realm, in the glory of His transcendent unity, and the splendors of His holy grandeur.

—Bahá'u'lláh

4 O Lord! The tongue of my tongue and the heart of my heart and the spirit of my spirit and my outward and inmost beings bear witness to Thy unity and Thy oneness, Thy power and Thine omnipotence, Thy grandeur and Thy sovereignty . . .

—Bahá'u'lláh

5 This is the Day that hath been illumined by the effulgent light of the Countenance of God—the Day when the Tongue of Grandeur is calling aloud: The Kingdom is God's, the Lord of the Day of Resurrection.

—Bahá'u'lláh

6 Give Thou ear unto what the Tongue of Grandeur uttereth . . .

—Bahá'u'lláh

7 We call unto thee from beyond the sea of grandeur, upon the crimson land, above the horizon of tribulation. Verily, no God is there save Him, the Almighty, the Most Generous. Walk thou steadfastly in My Cause and follow not the ways of those who, upon attaining unto the object of their desire, denied God, the Lord of Lords.

—Bahá'u'lláh

8 Glory to Thee, O Thou Who art the Lord of all worlds, and the Beloved of all such as have recognized Thee! Thou seest me sitting under a sword hanging on a thread, and art well aware that in such a state I have not fallen short of my duty towards Thy Cause, nor failed to shed abroad Thy praise, and declare Thy virtues, and deliver all Thou hadst prescribed unto me in Thy Tablets.

Though the sword be ready to fall on my head, I call Thy loved ones with such a calling that the hearts are carried away towards the horizon of Thy majesty and grandeur.

Purge out thoroughly their ears, O my Lord, that they may hearken unto the sweet melodies that have ascended from the right hand of the throne of Thy glory.

—Bahá'u'lláh

9 I beseech Thee, O Thou Who art the Lord of the worlds, and the Beloved of such as have recognized Thee, and the Desire of all that are in heaven and on earth, by Thy Name through which the cry of every suppliant hath ascended into the heaven of Thy transcendent holiness, through which every seeker hath soared to the sublimities of Thy unity and grandeur, through which the imperfect have been perfected, and the abased exalted, and the tongue of every stammerer unloosed, and the sick made whole, and whatever was unworthy of Thy highness and beseemed not Thy greatness and Thy sovereignty made acceptable unto Thee,—I beseech Thee to aid us by Thine invisible hosts and by a company of the angels of Thy Cause.

Do Thou, then, accept the works we have performed for love of Thee, and for the sake of Thy pleasure. Cast us not away, O my God, from the door of Thy mercy, and break not our hopes in the wonders of Thy grace and favors.

—Bahá'u'lláh

10 My majesty is My gift to thee, and My grandeur the token of My mercy unto thee. That which beseemeth Me none shall understand, nor can anyone recount. Verily, I have preserved it in My hidden storehouses and in the treasuries of My command, as a sign of My loving-kindness unto My servants and My mercy unto My people.

—Bahá'u'lláh

11 Of old it hath been revealed: "Love of one's country is an element of the Faith of God."

The Tongue of Grandeur hath, however, in the day of His manifestation proclaimed: "It is not his to boast who loveth his country, but it is his who loveth the world."

Through the power released by these exalted words He hath lent a fresh impulse and set a new direction to the birds of men's hearts, and hath obliterated every trace of restriction and limitation from God's holy Book.

—Bahá'u'lláh

12 I bear witness that there is no God but Thee, inasmuch as Thou art invested with sovereignty, grandeur, glory and power which no one among Thy servants can visualize or comprehend.

—The Báb

13 I implore Thee by the splendor of the light of Thy glorious face, the majesty of Thine ancient grandeur and the power of Thy transcendent sovereignty to ordain for us at this moment every measure of that which is good and seemly and to destine for us every portion of the outpourings of Thy grace. For granting of gifts doth not cause Thee loss, nor doth the bestowing of favors diminish Thy wealth.

Glorified art Thou, O Lord! Verily I am poor while in truth Thou art rich; verily I am lowly while in truth Thou art mighty; verily I am impotent while in truth Thou art powerful; verily I am abased while in truth Thou art the most exalted; verily I am distressed while in truth Thou art the Lord of might.

—The Báb

14 Throughout eternity Thou hast been, O my Lord, and wilt ever remain the One true God, while all else save Thee are needy and poor. Having clung tenaciously to Thy Cord, O my God, I have detached myself from all mankind, and having set my face towards the habitation of Thy tender mercy, I have turned away from all created things.

Graciously inspire me, O my God, through Thy grace and bounty, Thy glory and majesty, and Thy dominion and grandeur, for no one mighty and all-knowing can I find beside Thee. Protect me, O my God, through the potency of Thy transcendent and all-sufficing glory and by the hosts of the heavens and the earth, inasmuch as in no one can I wholly place my trust but in Thee and no refuge is there but Thee.

—The Báb

15 O Lord, my God! Give me Thy grace to serve Thy loved ones, strengthen me in my servitude to Thee, illumine my brow with the light of adoration in Thy court of holiness, and of prayer to Thy Kingdom of grandeur.

—'Abdu'l-Bahá

16 And among His signs is the sublimity of His grandeur . . .

—'Abdu'l-Bahá

17 The consummation of this limitless universe with all its grandeur and glory hath been man himself . . .

—'Abdu'l-Bahá

18 Humanity is not perfect. There are imperfections in every human being, and you will always become unhappy if you look toward the people themselves. But if you look toward God, you will love them and be kind to them, for the world of God is the world of perfection and complete mercy.

Therefore, do not look at the shortcomings of anybody; see with the sight of forgiveness. The imperfect eye beholds imperfections. The eye that covers faults looks toward the Creator of souls. He created them, trains and provides for them, endows them with capacity and life, sight and hearing; therefore, they are the signs of His grandeur.

—'Abdu'l-Bahá

19 O God, my God!
How can I glorify or describe Thee inaccessible as Thou art; immeasurably high and sanctified art Thou above every description and praise.

O God, my God! Have mercy then upon my helpless state, my poverty, my misery, my abasement! Give me to drink from the generous cup of Thy grace and forgiveness, stir me with the sweet scents of Thy love, gladden my bosom with the light of Thy knowledge, purify my soul with the mysteries of Thy oneness, raise me to life with the gentle breeze that cometh from the gardens of Thy mercy—till I sever myself from all else but Thee, and lay hold of the hem of Thy garment of grandeur . . .

—'Abdu'l-Bahá

*H*e is God!
O Lord, my God, my Well-Beloved! These are servants of Thine that have heard Thy Voice, given ear to Thy Word and hearkened to Thy Call. They have believed in Thee, witnessed Thy wonders, acknowledged Thy proof and

testified to Thine evidence. They have walked in Thy ways, followed Thy guidance, discovered Thy mysteries, comprehended the secrets of Thy Book, the verses of Thy Scrolls and the tidings of Thy Epistles and Tablets. They have clung to the hem of Thy garment and held fast unto the robe of Thy light and grandeur. Their footsteps have been strengthened in Thy Covenant and their hearts made firm in Thy Testament.

Lord! Do Thou kindle in their hearts the flame of Thy divine attraction and grant that the bird of love and understanding may sing within their hearts. Grant that they may be even as potent signs, resplendent standards, and perfect as Thy Word. Exalt by them Thy Cause, unfurl Thy banners and publish far and wide Thy wonders. Make by them Thy Word triumphant, and strengthen the loins of Thy loved ones. Unloose their tongues to laud Thy Name, and inspire them to do Thy holy will and pleasure. Illumine their faces in Thy Kingdom of holiness, and perfect their joy by aiding them to arise for the triumph of Thy Cause.

—'Abdu'l-Bahá

Light

Núr

Darkness hath been chased away by the dawning-light of the mercy of thy Lord, the source of all light.
—Bahá'u'lláh

I Glorified art Thou, O God of all names and Creator of the heavens!

I render Thee thanks that Thou hast made known unto Thy servants this Day whereon the river that is life indeed hath flowed forth from the fingers of Thy bounty, and the springtime of Thy revelation and Thy presence hath appeared through Thy manifestation unto all who are in Thy heaven and all who are on Thy earth.

This is the Day, O my Lord, whose brightness Thou hast exalted above the brightness of the sun and the splendors thereof. I testify that the light it sheddeth proceedeth out of the glory of the light of Thy countenance, and is begotten by the radiance of the morn of Thy Revelation.

—Bahá'u'lláh

2 . . . every age requireth a fresh measure of the light of God.

—Bahá'u'lláh

3 Indeed He is a Light which is not followed by darkness . . .

—Bahá'u'lláh

4 Magnified be Thy name, O Lord my God!
I know not what the water is with which Thou hast created me, or what the fire Thou hast kindled within me, or the clay wherewith Thou hast kneaded me. The restlessness of every sea hath been stilled, but not the restlessness of this Ocean which moveth at the bidding of the winds of Thy will. The flame of every fire hath been extinguished except the Flame which the hands of Thine omnipotence have kindled, and whose radiance Thou hast, by the power of Thy name, shed abroad before all that are in Thy heaven and all that are on Thy earth. As the tribulations deepen, it waxeth hotter and hotter.

Behold, then, O my God, how Thy Light hath been compassed with the onrushing winds of Thy decree, how the tempests that blow and beat upon it from every side have added to its brightness and increased its splendor.

For all this let Thee be praised.

—Bahá'u'lláh

5 Peerless is this Day, for it is as the eye to past ages and centuries, and as a light unto the darkness of the times.

—Bahá'u'lláh

6 O people of Justice!
Be as brilliant as the light, and as splendid as the fire that blazed in the Burning Bush. The brightness of the fire of your love will no doubt fuse and unify the contending peoples and kindreds of the earth, whilst the fierceness of the flame of enmity and hatred cannot but result in strife and ruin. We beseech God that He may shield His creatures from the evil designs of His enemies. He verily hath power over all things.

—Bahá'u'lláh

7 O Son of Spirit!
With the joyful tidings of light I hail thee: rejoice! To the court of holiness I summon thee; abide therein that thou mayest live in peace for evermore.

—Bahá'u'lláh

8 O Son of Being!
Thou art My lamp and My light is in thee. Get thou from it thy radiance and seek none other than Me.

—Bahá'u'lláh

9 O Son of Man!

The light hath shone on thee from the horizon of the sacred Mount and the spirit of enlightenment hath breathed in the Sinai of thy heart. Wherefore, free thyself from the veils of idle fancies and enter into My court, that thou mayest be fit for everlasting life and worthy to meet Me. Thus may death not come upon thee, neither weariness nor trouble.

—Bahá'u'lláh

10 Verily, I say, so fierce is the blaze of the Bush of love, burning in the Sinai of the heart, that the streaming waters of holy utterance can never quench its flame. Oceans can never allay this Leviathan's burning thirst, and this Phoenix of the undying fire can abide nowhere save in the glow of the countenance of the Well-Beloved.

Therefore, O brother! kindle with the oil of wisdom the lamp of the spirit within the innermost chamber of thy heart, and guard it with the globe of understanding, that the breath of the infidel may extinguish not its flame nor dim its brightness. Thus have We illuminated the heavens of utterance with the splendors of the Sun of divine wisdom and understanding, that thy heart may find peace, that thou mayest be of those who, on the wings of certitude, have soared unto the heaven of the love of their Lord, the All-Merciful.

—Bahá'u'lláh

11 By the righteousness of God! The Dawn hath truly brightened and the light hath shone forth and the night hath receded. Happy are they that comprehend. Happy are they that have attained thereunto.

—Bahá'u'lláh

12 O peoples of the earth!
Verily the resplendent Light of God hath appeared in your midst, invested with this unerring Book, that ye may be guided aright to the ways of peace and, by the leave of God, step out of the darkness into the light and onto this far-extended Path of Truth . . .

—The Báb

13 O Almighty! Look upon us with the glance of mercifulness. Grant us heavenly confirmation. Bestow upon us the breath of the Holy Spirit, so that we may be assisted in Thy service and, like unto brilliant stars, shine in these regions with the light of Thy guidance.

Verily, Thou art the Powerful, the Mighty, the Wise and the Seeing.

—'Abdu'l-Bahá

14 So far as ye are able, ignite a candle of love in every meeting, and with tenderness rejoice and cheer ye every heart.

—'Abdu'l-Bahá

15 O ye friends of God, redouble your efforts, strain every nerve, till ye triumph in your servitude to the Ancient Beauty, the Manifest Light, and become the cause of spreading far and wide the rays of the Day-Star of Truth. Breathe ye into the world's worn and wasted body the fresh breath of life, and in the furrows of every region sow ye holy seed.

Rise up to champion this Cause; open your lips and teach. In the meeting place of life be ye a guiding candle; in the skies of this world be dazzling stars; in the gardens of unity be birds of the spirit, singing of inner truths and mysteries.

—'Abdu'l-Bahá

16 These days are very precious; grasp the present opportunity and ignite a candle that shall never be extinguished, and which shall pour out its light eternally illuminating the world of mankind!

—'Abdu'l-Bahá

17 Universal benefits derive from the grace of the Divine religions, for they lead their true followers to sincerity of intent, to high purpose, to purity and spotless honor, to surpassing kindness and compassion, to the keeping of their covenants when they have covenanted, to concern for the rights of others, to liberality, to justice in every aspect of life, to humanity and philanthropy, to valor and to unflagging efforts in the service of mankind.

It is religion, to sum up, which produces all human virtues, and it is these virtues which are the bright candles of civilization.

—'Abdu'l-Bahá

18 Thus may each one of you be even as a candle casting its light, the center of attraction wherever people come together . . .

—'Abdu'l-Bahá

19 Now is the time for the faithful friends of 'Abdu'l-Bahá, who have been the recipients of the Glorious Light, to shine forth even as brilliant stars. The radiance of our Faith must be such as to dispel the clouds of doubt and guide the world to the Day-spring of Truth.

—The Greatest Holy Leaf

In cycles gone by, though harmony was established, yet, owing to the absence of means, the unity of all mankind could not have been achieved. Continents remained widely divided, nay even among the peoples of one and the same continent association and interchange of thought were well-nigh impossible. Consequently intercourse, understanding and unity amongst all the peoples and kindreds of the earth *were unattainable. In this day, however, means of communication have multiplied, and the five continents of the earth have virtually merged into one. And for everyone it is now easy to travel to any land, to associate and exchange views with its peoples, and to become familiar, through publications, with the conditions, the religious beliefs and the thoughts of all men.*

In like manner all the members of the human family, whether peoples or governments, cities or villages, have become increasingly interdependent. For none is self-sufficiency any longer possible, inasmuch as political ties unite all peoples and nations, and the bonds of trade and industry, of agriculture and education, are being strengthened every day. Hence the unity of all mankind can in this day be achieved. Verily this is none other but one of the wonders of this wondrous age, this glorious century. Of this past ages have been deprived, for this century—the century of light—hath been endowed with unique and unprecedented glory, power and illumination. Hence the miraculous unfolding of a fresh marvel every day. Eventually it will be seen how bright its candles will burn in the assemblage of man.

Behold how its light is now dawning upon the world's darkened horizon.

The first candle is unity in the political realm, the early glimmerings of which can now be discerned.

The second candle is unity of thought in world undertakings, the consummation of which will erelong be witnessed.

The third candle is unity in freedom which will surely come to pass.

The fourth candle is unity in religion which is the cornerstone of the foundation itself, and which, by the power of God, will be revealed in all its splendor.

The fifth candle is the unity of nations—a unity which in this century will be securely established, causing all the peoples of the world to regard themselves as citizens of one common fatherland.

The sixth candle is unity of races, making of all that dwell on earth peoples and kindreds of one race.

The seventh candle is unity of language, i.e., the choice of a universal tongue in which all peoples will be instructed and converse.

Each and every one of these will inevitably come to pass, inasmuch as the power of the Kingdom of God will aid and assist in their realization.

—'Abdu'l-Bahá

Mercy

Raḥmat

. . . rivers of mercy have streamed from His Pen . . .
—Bahá'u'lláh

1 Thou art the Lord of the worlds, and of all those who show mercy, art the Most Merciful.

—Bahá'u'lláh

2 This Day a door is open wider than both heaven and earth. The eye of the mercy of Him Who is the Desire of the worlds is turned towards all men.

—Bahá'u'lláh

3 I beseech Thee, O my Lord, by Thy mercy that hath surpassed the entire creation, and Thy generosity that hath embraced all created things, to cause me to turn my face wholly towards Thee, and to seek Thy shel-

47

ter, and to be steadfast in my love for Thee. Write down, then, for me what Thou didst ordain for them who love Thee.

Powerful art Thou to do what Thou pleasest. No God is there beside Thee, the Ever-Forgiving, the All-Bountiful.

—Bahá'u'lláh

4 Have mercy, then, upon me, O my Lord, through Thy gracious providence and generosity, and incline mine ear to the sweet melodies of the birds that warble their praise of Thee, amidst the branches of the tree of Thy oneness.

Thou art the Great Giver, the Ever-Forgiving, the Most Compassionate.

—Bahá'u'lláh

5 Praised be Thou, O Lord our God, inasmuch as Thou hast enabled us to recognize Thy most exalted and all-glorious Self. We will, by Thy mercy, cleave to Thee, and will detach ourselves from any one but Thee. We have realized that Thou art the Beloved of the worlds and the Creator of earth and heaven!

Glorified be God, the Lord of all creation!

—Bahá'u'lláh

6 Cast not out, I entreat Thee, O my Lord, them that have sought Thee, and turn not away such as have directed their steps towards Thee, and deprive not of

Thy grace all that love Thee. Thou art He, O my Lord, Who hath called Himself the God of Mercy, the Most Compassionate. Have mercy, then, upon Thy handmaiden who hath sought Thy shelter, and set her face towards Thee.

Thou art, verily, the Ever-Forgiving, the Most Merciful.

—Bahá'u'lláh

7 O Son of Bounty!

Out of the wastes of nothingness, with the clay of My command I made thee to appear, and have ordained for thy training every atom in existence and the essence of all created things. Thus, ere thou didst issue from thy mother's womb, I destined for thee two founts of gleaming milk, eyes to watch over thee, and hearts to love thee. Out of My loving-kindness, 'neath the shade of My mercy I nurtured thee, and guarded thee by the essence of My grace and favor. And My purpose in all this was that thou mightest attain My everlasting dominion and become worthy of My invisible bestowals.

—Bahá'u'lláh

8 O Son of Man!

My calamity is My providence, outwardly it is fire and vengeance, but inwardly it is light and mercy. Hasten thereunto that thou mayest become an eternal light and an immortal spirit. This is My command unto thee, do thou observe it.

—Bahá'u'lláh

9 O ye peoples of the world!
Know assuredly that My commandments are the lamps of My loving providence among My servants, and the keys of My mercy for My creatures. Thus hath it been sent down from the heaven of the Will of your Lord, the Lord of Revelation.

—Bahá'u'lláh

10 The Ancient Beauty hath consented to be bound with chains that mankind may be released from its bondage, and hath accepted to be made a prisoner within this most mighty Stronghold that the whole world may attain unto true liberty. He hath drained to its dregs the cup of sorrow, that all the peoples of the earth may attain unto abiding joy, and be filled with gladness. This is of the mercy of your Lord, the Compassionate, the Most Merciful. We have accepted to be abased, O believers in the Unity of God, that ye may be exalted, and have suffered manifold afflictions, that ye might prosper and flourish.

—Bahá'u'lláh

11 Shield, I pray Thee, O my Beloved, my heart's Desire, Thy servant who hath sought Thy face . . . Cause him, then, to be wholly devoted to Thee, to declare Thy name, and to fix his gaze upon the sanctuary of Thy Revelation.

Thou art, in truth, He Who, at no time, hath turned away those who have set their hopes in Thee from the

door of Thy mercy, nor prevented such as have sought
Thee from attaining the court of Thy grace.

No God is there but Thee, the Most Powerful, the
All-Highest, the Help in Peril, the All-Glorious, the
All-Compelling, the Unconditioned.

—Bahá'u'lláh

12 Assuredly no God is there other than Him, the
All-Possessing, the Most Generous. The revela-
tions of His bounty pervade all created things; He is the
Merciful, the Compassionate.

—The Báb

13 Glorified and exalted art Thou, and praise be unto
Thee for whatsoever Thou lovest and desirest, and
thanks be unto Thee for that which Thou hast decreed
and preordained. From time immemorial Thy tender
mercy hath been sent down and the process of Thy creation hath been and ever is ceaseless. Thy handiwork is
unlike the work of anyone besides Thee, and Thy goodly
gifts are unparalleled by the gifts of anyone other than
Thyself.

Praise be unto Thee, O My Beloved, and magnified
be Thy Name.

—The Báb

14 O Lord! Whether traveling or at home, and in my
occupation or in my work, I place my whole trust
in Thee.

Grant me then Thy sufficing help so as to make me independent of all things, O Thou Who art unsurpassed in Thy mercy!

—The Báb

15 It is better to guide one soul than to possess all that is on earth, for as long as that guided soul is under the shadow of the Tree of Divine Unity, he and the one who hath guided him will both be recipients of God's tender mercy, whereas possession of earthly things will cease at the time of death.

The path to guidance is one of love and compassion, not of force and coercion. This hath been God's method in the past, and shall continue to be in the future! He causeth him whom He pleaseth to enter the shadow of His Mercy. Verily, He is the Supreme Protector, the All-Generous.

—The Báb

16 . . . God "sendeth rain on the just and on the unjust"—that is to say, the mercy of God is universal.

— 'Abdu'l-Bahá

17 The Fatherhood of God, His loving-kindness and beneficence are apparent to all. In His mercy He provides fully and amply for His creatures, and if any soul sins, He does not suspend His bounty. All created things are visible manifestations of His Fatherhood, mercy and heavenly bestowals.

Human brotherhood is, likewise, as clear and evident as the sun, for all are servants of one God, belong to one humankind, inhabit the same globe, are sheltered beneath the overshadowing dome of heaven and submerged in the sea of divine mercy.

—'Abdu'l-Bahá

18 Oh, friends of God, be living examples of justice! So that by the Mercy of God, the world may see in your actions that you manifest the attributes of justice and mercy.

—'Abdu'l-Bahá

19 O my God! O my God!
Verily, these are servants at the threshold of Thy mercy, and maidservants at the door of Thy oneness. Verily, they have gathered in this temple to turn to Thy face of glory, holding to the hem of Thy garment and to Thy singleness, seeking Thy good pleasure and ascent into Thy Kingdom. They receive effulgence from the Sun of Reality in this glorious century, and they long for Thy goodwill in all great affairs. O Lord! Illumine their sight with a vision of Thy signs and riches, and quicken their ears with hearkening to Thy Word. Render their hearts replete with Thy love, and gladden

their spirits with Thy meeting. Deign to bestow upon them spiritual good in Thine earth and heaven, and make them signs of unity among Thy servants in order that the real unity may appear and all may become one in Thy Cause and Kingdom.

Verily, Thou art the Generous. Verily, Thou art the Mighty, the Spiritual. Thou art the Merciful, the Clement.

—'Abdu'l-Bahá

The foundation principles of the teachings of Christ were mercy, love, fellowship, benevolence, altruism, the resplendence or radiance of divine bestowals, acquisition of the breaths of the Holy Spirit and oneness with God. Furthermore, . . . Christ declared that the Father "maketh his sun to rise on the evil and on the good, and sendeth rain on the just and on the unjust." The meaning of this declaration is that the mercy of God encircles all mankind, that not a single individual is deprived of the mercy of God, and no soul is denied the resplendent bestowals of God.

The whole human race is submerged in the sea of the mercy of the Lord, and we are all the sheep of the one divine Shepherd. Whatever shortcomings exist among us must be remedied. For example, those who are ignorant must be educated so that they may become wise; the sick must be treated until they recover; those who are immature must be trained in order to reach maturity; those asleep must be awakened. All this must be accomplished through love and not through hatred and hostility.

Furthermore, Jesus Christ, referring to the prophecy of Isaiah, spoke of those who having eyes, see not, having ears, hear not, having hearts, understand not; yet they were to be healed. Therefore, it is evident that the bounties of Christ transformed the eye which was blind into a seeing one, rendered the ear which was formerly deaf, attentive, and made the hard, callous heart tender and sensitive. In other words, the meaning is that although the people possess external eyes, yet the insight, or perception, of the soul is blind; although the outer ear hears, the spiritual hearing is deaf; although they possess conscious hearts, they are without illumination; and the bounties of Christ save souls from these conditions.

It is evident, then, that the manifestation of the Messiah was synonymous with universal mercy. His providence was universal, and His teachings were for all. His lights were not restricted to a few. Every Christ came to the world of mankind.

—'Abdu'l-Bahá

WORDS

Kalimát

Within every word a new spirit is hidden.
—Bahá'u'lláh

1 The Book of God is wide open, and His Word is summoning mankind unto Him.
—Bahá'u'lláh

2 Through the power of the words He hath uttered the whole of the human race can be illumined with the light of unity . . .
—Bahá'u'lláh

3 I testify that no sooner had the First Word proceeded, through the potency of Thy will and purpose, out of His mouth, and the First Call gone forth

from His lips than the whole creation was revolution-ized, and all that are in the heavens and all that are on earth were stirred to the depths. Through that Word the realities of all created things were shaken, were divided, separated, scattered, combined and reunited, disclosing, in both the contingent world and the heavenly king-dom, entities of a new creation, and revealing, in the unseen realms, the signs and tokens of Thy unity and oneness. Through that Call Thou didst announce unto all Thy servants the advent of Thy most great Revelation and the appearance of Thy most perfect Cause.

—Bahá'u'lláh

4 I implore Thee, O my God, by Thy Most Great Name, to enrapture the nations through the potency of the Word which Thou didst ordain to be the king of all words, the Word whereby the goodly pearls of Thy hidden wisdom were uncovered, and the gem-like mysteries which were wrapped up within Thee were unraveled. Deprive them not, by Thy grace and bounty, of the things Thou didst desire for them, and suffer them not to be far removed from the shores of the ocean of Thy presence.

—Bahá'u'lláh

5 Thou didst call me into being, O my God, to exalt Thy Word . . .

—Bahá'u'lláh

6 O friend of mine!

The Word of God is the king of words and its pervasive influence is incalculable. It hath ever dominated and will continue to dominate the realm of being.

The Great Being saith: The Word is the master key for the whole world, inasmuch as through its potency the doors of the hearts of men, which in reality are the doors of heaven, are unlocked. No sooner had but a glimmer of its effulgent splendor shone forth upon the mirror of love than the blessed word "I am the Best-Beloved" was reflected therein. It is an ocean inexhaustible in riches, comprehending all things. Every thing which can be perceived is but an emanation therefrom.

—Bahá'u'lláh

7 O Children of Adam!

Holy words and pure and goodly deeds ascend unto the heaven of celestial glory.

—Bahá'u'lláh

8 Guidance hath ever been given by words, and now it is given by deeds. Every one must show forth deeds that are pure and holy, for words are the property of all alike, whereas such deeds as these belong only to Our loved ones. Strive then with heart and soul to distinguish yourselves by your deeds. In this wise We counsel you in this holy and resplendent tablet.

—Bahá'u'lláh

9 Say, O brethren! Let deeds, not words, be your adorning.

—Bahá'u'lláh

10 O My Friends!
Have ye forgotten that true and radiant morn, when in those hallowed and blessed surroundings ye were all gathered in My presence beneath the shade of the tree of life, which is planted in the all-glorious paradise? Awe-struck ye listened as I gave utterance to these three most holy words: O friends! Prefer not your will to Mine, never desire that which I have not desired for you, and approach Me not with lifeless hearts, defiled with worldly desires and cravings. Would ye but sanctify your souls, ye would at this present hour recall that place and those surroundings, and the truth of My utterance should be made evident unto all of you.

—Bahá'u'lláh

11 The Word of God may be likened unto a sapling, whose roots have been implanted in the hearts of men. It is incumbent upon you to foster its growth through the living waters of wisdom, of sanctified and holy words, so that its root may become firmly fixed and its branches may spread out as high as the heavens and beyond.

—Bahá'u'lláh

12 Cleave unto that which draweth you together and uniteth you. This, verily, is the most exalted Word which the Mother Book hath sent down and revealed unto you.

—Bahá'u'lláh

13 Ye are the letters of the words, and the words of the Book.

—Bahá'u'lláh

14 No man of wisdom can demonstrate his knowledge save by means of words. This showeth the significance of the Word as is affirmed in all the Scriptures, whether of former times or more recently. For it is through its potency and animating spirit that the people of the world have attained so eminent a position.

—Bahá'u'lláh

15 One word is like unto springtime causing the tender saplings of the rose-garden of knowledge to become verdant and flourishing, while another word is even as a deadly poison. It behoveth a prudent man of wisdom to speak with utmost leniency and forbearance so that the sweetness of his words may induce everyone to attain that which befitteth man's station.

—Bahá'u'lláh

16 Take heed to carefully consider the words of every soul, then hold fast to the proofs which attest the truth. If ye fail to discover truth in a person's words, make them not the object of contention, inasmuch as ye have been forbidden in the Bayán to enter into idle disputation and controversy . . .

—The Báb

17 Beware lest ye harm any soul, or make any heart to sorrow; lest ye wound any man with your words, be he known to you or a stranger, be he friend or foe. Pray ye for all; ask ye that all be blessed, all be forgiven.

— 'Abdu'l-Bahá

18 O handmaid of God, peace must first be established among individuals, until it leadeth in the end to peace among nations.

Wherefore, O ye Bahá'ís, strive ye with all your might to create, through the power of the Word of God, genuine love, spiritual communion and durable bonds among individuals. This is your task.

—'Abdu'l-Bahá

19 Now is the time for the lovers of God to raise high the banners of unity, to intone, in the assemblages of the world, the verses of friendship and love and to demonstrate to all that the grace of God is one. Thus will the tabernacles of holiness be upraised on the summits of the earth, gathering all peoples into the protective shadow of the Word of Oneness.

— 'Abdu'l-Bahá

*W*hen the channel of the human soul is cleansed of all worldly and impeding attachments, it will unfailingly perceive the breath of the Beloved across immeasurable distances, and will, led by its perfume, attain and enter the City of Certitude. Therein he will discern the wonders of His ancient wisdom, and will perceive all the hidden teachings from the rustling leaves of the Tree—which flourisheth in that City. With both his inner and his outer ear he will hear from its dust the hymns of glory and praise ascending unto the Lord of Lords, and with his inner eye will he discover the mysteries of "return" and "revival."

How unspeakably glorious are the signs, the tokens, the revelations, and splendors which He Who is the King of names and attributes hath destined for that City! The attainment of this City quencheth thirst without water, and kindleth the love of God without fire. Within every blade of grass are enshrined the mysteries of an inscrutable wisdom, and upon every rose-bush a myriad nightingales pour out, in blissful rapture, their melody. Its wondrous tulips unfold the mystery of the undying Fire in the Burning Bush, and its sweet savors of holiness breathe the perfume of the Messianic Spirit. It bestoweth wealth without gold, and conferreth immortality without death. In every leaf ineffable delights are treasured, and within every chamber unnumbered mysteries lie hidden.

. . . Once in about a thousand years shall this City be renewed and re-adorned.

Wherefore, O my friend, it behooveth Us to exert the highest endeavor to attain unto that City, and, by the grace of God and His loving-kindness, rend asunder the "veils of glory"; so that, with inflexible steadfastness, we may sacrifice our drooping souls in the path of the New Beloved. We should with tearful eyes, fervently and repeatedly, implore Him to grant us the favor of that grace.

That city is none other than the Word of God revealed in every age and dispensation. In the days of Moses it was the Pentateuch; in the days of Jesus the Gospel; in the days of Muhammad the Messenger of God the Qur'an; in this day the Bayán; and in the dispensation of Him Whom God will make manifest His own Book—the Book unto which all the Books of former Dispensations must needs be referred, the Book which standeth amongst them all transcendent and supreme.

—Bahá'u'lláh

Perfection

Kamál

Every other perfection is as naught in face of His consummate perfection . . ..
—The Báb

1 By the righteousness of the Almighty! The measure of the favors of God hath been filled up, His Word hath been perfected . . .

—Bahá'u'lláh

2 So perfect and comprehensive is His creation that no mind nor heart, however keen or pure, can ever grasp the nature of the most insignificant of His creatures; much less fathom the mystery of Him Who is the Day Star of Truth, Who is the invisible and unknowable Essence.

—Bahá'u'lláh

3 O Son of Being!
With the hands of power I made thee and with the fingers of strength I created thee; and within thee have I placed the essence of My light. Be thou content with it and seek naught else, for My work is perfect and My command is binding. Question it not, nor have a doubt thereof.

—Bahá'u'lláh

4 Know thou, that I have wafted unto thee all the fragrances of holiness, have fully revealed to thee My word, have perfected through thee My bounty and have desired for thee that which I have desired for My Self. Be then content with My pleasure and thankful unto Me.

—Bahá'u'lláh

5 With fixed and steady gaze, born of the unerring eye of God, scan for a while the horizon of divine knowledge, and contemplate those words of perfection which the Eternal hath revealed, that haply the mysteries of divine wisdom, hidden ere now beneath the veil of glory and treasured within the tabernacle of His grace, may be made manifest unto you.

—Bahá'u'lláh

6 The spirit that animateth the human heart is the knowledge of God, and its truest adorning is the recognition of the truth that "He doeth whatsoever He

willeth, and ordaineth that which He pleaseth." Its raiment is the fear of God, and its perfection steadfastness in His Faith. Thus God instructeth whosoever seeketh Him.

—Bahá'u'lláh

7 The time hath come for the effects and perfections of the Most Great Name to be made manifest in this excellent age, so as to establish, beyond any doubt, that this era is the era of Baha'u'llah, and this age is distinguished above all other ages.

—'Abdu'l-Bahá

8 Know that the attributes of perfection, the splendor of the divine bounties, and the lights of inspiration are visible and evident in all the Holy Manifestations . . .

—'Abdu'l-Bahá

9 As to the Holy Manifestations of God, They are the focal points where the signs, tokens and perfections of that sacred, pre-existent Reality appear in all their splendor. They are an eternal grace, a heavenly glory, and on them dependeth the everlasting life of humankind.

—'Abdu'l-Bahá

10 Man is . . . the end of imperfection and the beginning of perfection.

—'Abdu'l-Bahá

11 Man is the highest species because he is the possessor of the perfections of all the classes—that is, he has a body which grows and which feels. As well as having the perfections of the mineral, of the vegetable and of the animal, he also possesses an especial excellence which the other beings are without—that is, the intellectual perfections. Therefore, man is the most noble of beings.

—'Abdu'l-Bahá

12 . . . with the human soul, there is no decline. Its only movement is towards perfection; growth and progress alone constitute the motion of the soul.

Divine perfection is infinite, therefore the progress of the soul is also infinite.

—'Abdu'l-Bahá

13 O ye friends of God!

Because, in this most momentous of ages, the Sun of Truth [Bahá'u'lláh] hath risen at the highest point of the spring equinox, and cast its rays on every clime, it shall kindle such tremulous excitement, it shall release such vibrations in the world of being, it shall stimulate such growth and development, it shall stream out with such a glory of light, and clouds of grace shall pour down such plentiful waters, and fields and plains shall teem with such a galaxy of sweet-smelling plants and blooms, that this lowly earth will become the Abhá Kingdom, and this nether world the world above. Then will this fleck of dust be as the vast circle of the skies, this human place the palace-court of God, this spot of clay the dayspring of the endless favors of the Lord of Lords.

Wherefore, O loved ones of God! Make ye a mighty effort till you yourselves betoken this advancement and all these confirmations, and become focal centers of God's blessings, daysprings of the light of His unity, promoters of the gifts and graces of civilized life. Be ye in that land vanguards of the perfections of humankind . . .

—'Abdu'l-Bahá

14 Every imperfect soul is self-centered and thinketh only of his own good. But as his thoughts expand a little he will begin to think of the welfare and comfort of his family. If his ideas still more widen, his concern will be the felicity of his fellow citizens; and if still they widen, he will be thinking of the glory of his land and of his race.

But when ideas and views reach the utmost degree of expansion and attain the stage of perfection, then will he be interested in the exaltation of humankind. He will then be the well-wisher of all men and the seeker of the weal and prosperity of all lands. This is indicative of perfection.

—'Abdu'l-Bahá

15 Thou must endeavor greatly so that thou mayest become unique in thy profession and famous in those parts, because attaining perfection in one's profession in this merciful period is considered to be worship of God. And whilst thou art occupied with thy profession, thou canst remember the True One.

—'Abdu'l-Bahá

16 If actions took the place of words, the world's misery would very soon be changed into comfort. A man who does great good, and talks not of it, is on the way to perfection.

—'Abdu'l-Bahá

17 Those who suffer most, attain to the greatest perfection.

—'Abdu'l-Bahá

18 He is the Compassionate, the All-Bountiful!
O God, my God! Thou seest me, Thou knowest me; Thou art my Haven and my Refuge. None have I sought nor any will I seek save Thee; no path have I

trodden nor any will I tread but the path of Thy love. In the darksome night of despair, my eye turneth expectant and full of hope to the morn of Thy boundless favor and at the hour of dawn my drooping soul is refreshed and strengthened in remembrance of Thy beauty and perfection. He whom the grace of Thy mercy aideth, though he be but a drop, shall become the boundless ocean, and the merest atom which the outpouring of Thy loving-kindness assisteth, shall shine even as the radiant star.

Shelter under Thy protection, O Thou Spirit of purity, Thou Who art the All-Bountiful Provider, this enthralled, enkindled servant of Thine. Aid him in this world of being to remain steadfast and firm in Thy love and grant that this broken-winged bird attain a refuge and shelter in Thy divine nest that abideth upon the celestial tree.

—'Abdu'l-Bahá

19 It is my heartfelt prayer that each one of you may attain to this perfect joy!

—'Abdu'l-Bahá

The first attribute of perfection is learning and the cultural attainments of the mind . . .

The second attribute of perfection is justice and impartiality. This means to have no regard for one's own personal *benefits and selfish advantages, and to carry out the laws of God without the slightest concern for anything else. It means to see one's self as only one of the servants of God, the All-Possessing, and except for aspiring to spiritual distinction, never attempting to be singled out from the others. It means to consider the welfare of the community as one's own. It means, in brief, to regard humanity as a single individual, and one's own self as a member of that corporeal form, and to know of a certainty that if pain or injury afflicts any member of that body, it must inevitably result in suffering for all the rest.*

The third requirement of perfection is to arise with complete sincerity and purity of purpose to educate the masses: to exert the utmost effort to instruct them in the various branches of learning and useful sciences, to encourage the development of modern progress, to widen the scope of commerce, industry and the arts, to further such measures as will increase the people's wealth. . . .

Other attributes of perfection are to fear God, to love God by loving His servants, to exercise mildness and forbearance and calm, to be sincere, amenable, clement and compassionate; to have resolution and courage, trustworthiness and energy, to strive and struggle, to be generous, loyal, without malice, to have zeal and a sense of honor, to be high-minded and magnanimous, and to have regard for the rights of others. Whoever is lacking in these excellent human qualities is defective.

—'Abdu'l-Bahá

Names

Asmá'

. . . make your hearts the daysprings of His exalted Names as recorded in the Book . . .
—The Báb

1 Glorified be Thy name, O Thou Who art the King of all Kings!

—Bahá'u'lláh

2 He Who is the sovereign Lord of all is come. The Kingdom is God's, the omnipotent Protector, the Self-Subsisting. Worship none but God, and, with radiant hearts, lift up your faces unto your Lord, the Lord of all names.

—Bahá'u'lláh

3 O my Lord, my Best-Beloved, the Mover of my actions, the Lode Star of my soul, the Voice that crieth in mine inmost being, the Object of mine heart's adoration! Praise be to Thee for having enabled me to turn my face towards Thee, for having set my soul ablaze through remembrance of Thee, for having aided Me to proclaim Thy Name and to sing Thy praises.

—Bahá'u'lláh

4 Magnified be Thy name, O Thou that forgivest the heedless ones that trespass against Thee!

—Bahá'u'lláh

5 Lauded be Thy name, O Thou Who beholdest all things and art hidden from all things!

—Bahá'u'lláh

6 Praised be Thou, O Lord my God!
I implore Thee, by Thy Most Great Name through Which Thou didst stir up Thy servants and build up Thy cities, and by Thy most excellent titles, and Thy most august attributes, to assist Thy people to turn in the direction of Thy manifold bounties, and set their faces towards the Tabernacle of Thy wisdom.

Heal Thou the sicknesses that have assailed the souls on every side, and have deterred them from directing their gaze towards the Paradise that lieth in the shelter of Thy shadowing Name, which Thou didst ordain to be the King of all names unto all who are in heaven and all who are on earth.

Potent art Thou to do as pleaseth Thee. In Thy hands is the empire of all names. There is none other God but Thee, the Mighty, the Wise.

—Bahá'u'lláh

7 O peoples of the world! Give ear unto the call of Him Who is the Lord of Names . . .

—Bahá'u'lláh

8 Lauded be Thy name, O Thou in Whose hands is the kingdom of all names, and in the grasp of Whose might are all that are in heaven and all that are on earth! I entreat Thee, by Him Who is Thy Most Effulgent Name Whom Thou hast made a target for the darts of Thy decree in Thy path, O Thou the King of eternity, to rend asunder the veils that have shut off Thy creatures from the horizon of Thy glory, that haply they may turn their faces in the direction of Thy mercy, and draw nigh unto the Day-Spring of Thy loving-kindness.

—Bahá'u'lláh

9 It beseemeth all men, in this Day, to take firm hold on the Most Great Name, and to establish the unity of all mankind. There is no place to flee to, no refuge that any one can seek, except Him.

—Bahá'u'lláh

10 Whatever is in the heavens and whatever is on the earth is a direct evidence of the revelation within it of the attributes and names of God, inasmuch as within every atom are enshrined the signs that bear eloquent testimony to the revelation of that Most Great Light.

—Bahá'u'lláh

11 Upon the inmost reality of each and every created thing He hath shed the light of one of His names, and made it a recipient of the glory of one of His attributes. Upon the reality of man, however, He hath focused the radiance of all of His names and attributes, and made it a mirror of His own Self. Alone of all created things man hath been singled out for so great a favor, so enduring a bounty.

—Bahá'u'lláh

12 I entreat Thee, O Thou Who art the Ruler of the kingdoms of creation and the Author of all names, to write down my name with the names of them who, from eternity, have circled round the Tabernacle of Thy majesty, and clung to the hem of Thy loving-kindness, and held fast the cord of Thy tender mercy.

Thou art, in truth, the Help in Peril, the Self-Subsisting.

—Bahá'u'lláh

13 If thou art sailing upon the sea of God's Names, which are reflected in all things, know thou that He is exalted and sanctified from being known through His creatures, or being described by His servants.

—The Báb

14 How shall we know God? We know Him by His attributes. We know Him by His signs. We know Him by His names.

—'Abdu'l-Bahá

15 The sovereignty, power, names, and attributes of God are eternal, ancient. His names presuppose creation and predicate His existence and will. We say God is Creator. This name Creator appears when we connote creation. We say God is the Provider. This name presupposes and proves the existence of the provided. God is Love. This name proves the existence of the beloved. In the same way God is Mercy, God is Justice, God is Life . . .

—'Abdu'l-Bahá

16 . . . for the names of God are actually and forever existing and not potential. Because they convey life, they are called Life-giving; because they provide, they are called Bountiful, the Provider; because they create, they are called Creator; because they educate and

govern, the name Lord God is applied. That is to say, the divine names emanate from the eternal attributes of Divinity.

—'Abdu'l-Bahá

17 The world, indeed each existing being, proclaims to us one of the names of God, but the reality of man is the collective reality, the general reality, and is the center where the glory of all the perfections of God shine forth—that is to say, for each name, each attribute, each perfection which we affirm of God there exists a sign in man.

—'Abdu'l-Bahá

18 . . . the attributes and the names of God shall be resplendent in the mirror of the reality of man, and the holy verse "We will make man in Our image and likeness" shall be realized.

—'Abdu'l-Bahá

19 When . . . thou dost contemplate the innermost essence of all things, and the individuality of each, thou wilt behold the signs of thy Lord's mercy in every created thing, and see the spreading rays of His Names and Attributes throughout all the realm of being, with evidences which none will deny save the froward and the unaware. Then wilt thou observe that the universe is a scroll that discloseth His hidden secrets, which are preserved in the well-guarded Tablet. And not an atom of all the atoms in existence, not a creature from amongst the creatures but speaketh His praise and telleth of His attributes and names, revealeth the glory of His might and guideth to His oneness and His mercy . . .

—'Abdu'l-Bahá

Glorified art Thou, O Lord my God!
I beseech Thee by Thy Name, the Restrainer, to withhold from us the maleficence of Thine adversaries who have disbelieved in Thy testimony, and caviled at Thy beauty. Overpower by Thy Name, the All-Subduing, such as have wronged Thy Previous Manifestation Who hath now appeared invested with Thy title, the All-Glorious. Lay hold, by Thy name, the Chastiser, on them that have treated Thy Cause with scorn, have jested at Thy most mighty utterances, and were hindered from attaining this most exalted station. Enable Thy loved ones, by Thy Name, the Victorious, to prevail against Thine enemies and the infidels among Thy creatures. Rend asunder, by Thy Name, the Cleaver, the veil that hideth the doings of them that have besmirched Thine honor and undermined Thy Faith among Thy people. Bind, by Thy Name, the Restorer, the broken

hearts of them that love Thee, and graciously bless them in their affairs. Teach them, by Thy Name, the All-Knowing, the wonders of Thy wisdom, that they may cleave steadfastly to Thy Faith and walk in the ways of Thy pleasure. Keep them safe, by Thy Name, the Withholder, from the tyranny of the oppressor and the wickedness of the evil-doers and the malice of the stirrers of mischief. Shield them, by Thy Name, the Preserver, within the stronghold of Thy might and power, that haply they may be protected from the darts of doubt that are hurled by such as have rebelled against Thee.

Sanctify for Thy servants, by Thy Name which Thou hast blessed above all other names, which Thou hast singled out for Thy favor, and by which Thou didst reveal Thy beauty, these days of which the Pen of Thy decree hath distinctly written, and which, according to Thy will and wisdom, have been preordained in Thine irrevocable Tablet.

Subject to Thy rule, by Thy Name, the Conqueror, the people of Thy realm, that all may turn towards Thy face and forsake their all for love of Thee and for the sake of Thy pleasure.

—Bahá'u'lláh

Might

'Izzat

*How great, how very great, is the power of His might that
encompasseth all worlds!*
—Bahá'u'lláh

1 Thou art the Possessor of power, and the King of
might. No God is there but Thee, the Strong, the
Unconstrained.

—Bahá'u'lláh

2 The door of grace hath been unlocked and He Who
is the Dayspring of Justice is come with perspicuous
signs and evident testimonies, from God, the Lord of
strength and of might!

—Bahá'u'lláh

3 All glory be unto the Lord of strength, might, and power!

None can withstand the operation of My will or the exercise of My might. I am He Who hath raised up all creatures through a word of My mouth, and My power is, in truth, equal to My purpose.

Say: It is in Our power, should We wish it, to cause all created things to expire in an instant, and, with the next, to endue them again with life. The knowledge thereof, however, is with God alone, the All-Knowing, the All-Informed.

It is in Our power, should We wish it, to enable a speck of floating dust to generate, in less than the twinkling of an eye, suns of infinite, of unimaginable splendor, to cause a dewdrop to develop into vast and numberless oceans, to infuse into every letter such force as to empower it to unfold all the knowledge of past and future ages.

—Bahá'u'lláh

4 I beseech Thee, O my Lord, by Thy most effulgent Name, to acquaint my people with the things Thou didst destine for them. . . . Uncover before them, O my Lord, the majesty of Thy Cause, lest they be led to doubt Thy sovereignty and the power of Thy might.

—Bahá'u'lláh

5 Sanctified be the Lord of all mankind, at the mention of Whose name all the atoms of the earth have been made to vibrate, and the Tongue of Grandeur hath been moved to disclose that which had been wrapt in His knowledge and lay concealed within the treasury of His might.

He, verily, through the potency of His name, the Mighty, the All-Powerful, the Most High, is the ruler of all that is in the heavens and all that is on earth.

—Bahá'u'lláh

6 Take Thou, O my God, the hands of such as have been drowned in the sea of idle fancies, and deliver them by Thy power and Thy sovereignty. Save them, then, with the arms of Thy might.

Powerful art Thou to do what Thou willest, and in Thy right hand are the reins of all that is in the heavens and all that is on earth.

—Bahá'u'lláh

7 Purify, O my God, the hearts of Thy creatures with the power of Thy sovereignty and might, that Thy words may sink deep into them.

—Bahá'u'lláh

8 I call on Thee O Mightiest One, O Sustaining One, O Potent One!

—Bahá'u'lláh

9 I implore Thee by the glory of Thy Manifestation and by the power of Thy might, Thy sovereignty and Thine exaltation to render victorious those who have arisen to serve Thee, who have aided Thy Cause and humbled themselves before the splendor of the light of Thy face.

—Bahá'u'lláh

10 I have committed, O my Lord, my spirit and my entire being into the right hand of Thy might and Thy protection, and I lay my head on my pillow through Thy power, and lift it up according to Thy will and Thy good-pleasure. Thou art, in truth, the Preserver, the Keeper, the Almighty, the Most Powerful.

By Thy might! I ask not, whether sleeping or waking, but that which Thou dost desire. I am Thy servant and in Thy hands. Do Thou graciously aid me to do what will shed forth the fragrance of Thy good pleasure. This, truly, is my hope and the hope of them that enjoy near access to Thee. Praised be Thou, O Lord of the worlds!

—Bahá'u'lláh

11 ... I bear witness that Thou art the Most Manifest, the Omnipotent, the Ever-Abiding; that of all things that exist on earth and in the heavens nothing whatsoever can frustrate Thy purpose and that Thou art the Knower of all things and the Lord of might and majesty.

—The Báb

12 He is the Almighty.

Glory be unto Him Who is the Lord of all that are in the heavens and on the earth; He is the All-Wise, the All-Informed. It is He Who calleth into being whatsoever He willeth at His behest; He is indeed the Clement, the Fashioner.

Say, verily He is equal to His purpose; whomsoever He willeth, He maketh victorious through the power of His hosts; there is none other God but Him, the Mighty, the Wise. His is the kingdom of earth and heaven and He is the Lord of power and glory. Such as have believed in God and in His signs are indeed the followers of truth and shall abide in the gardens of delight . . .

—The Báb

13 We are weak; He is mighty, because, were He not mighty, He could not have created us.

—'Abdu'l-Bahá

14 O God, my God!

I beg of Thee by the dawning of the light of Thy Beauty that hath illumined all the earth, and by the glance of Thy divine compassion's eye that considereth all things, and by the surging sea of Thy bestowals in which all things are immersed, and by Thy streaming clouds of bounty raining down gifts upon the essences of all created things, and by the splendors of Thy mercy

that existed before ever the world was — to help Thy
chosen ones to be faithful, and assist Thy loved ones to
serve at Thine exalted Threshold, and cause them to
gain the victory through the battalions of Thy might . . .

—'Abdu'l-Bahá

15 O Lord, Thou art the Almighty.
Thou art the Merciful. Thou art the Forgiver.
Thou art the Omnipotent.

—'Abdu'l-Bahá

16 O Lord!
Have pity on my weakness, and strengthen me
with Thy power. O Lord! Have pity on my impotence,
and assist me with Thy might and majesty.

—'Abdu'l-Bahá

17 . . . O Lord of Being, show forth Thy might and
Thy dominion.

—'Abdu'l-Bahá

18 We must look higher than all earthly thoughts;
detach ourselves from every material idea, crave
for the things of the spirit; fix our eyes on the everlasting

bountiful Mercy of the Almighty, who will fill our souls
with the gladness of joyful service to His command . . .

—'Abdu'l-Bahá

19 The divine Jerusalem has come down from
heaven. The bride of Zion has appeared. The
voice of the Kingdom of God has been raised. May you
attain supreme capacity and magnetic attraction in this
realm of might and power—manifesting new energy and
wonderful accomplishment, for God is your Assister and
Helper. The breath of the Holy Spirit is your comforter,
and the angels of heaven surround you.

—'Abdu'l-Bahá

*Verily Christ said "Come that I may make you fishers of
men" and today We say "Come, that We may make
you quickeners of the world" . . . Lo! This is the Day of
Grace! Come ye that I may make you the kings of the realm
of My Kingdom. If ye obey Me you will see that which We
have promised you, and I will make you the friends of My
Soul in the realm of My greatness and the Companions of My
Beauty in the heaven of My Might forever.*

—Bahá'u'lláh

WILL

Mashíyyat

*Thou art God, potent art Thou to do what Thou desirest. No one
can withstand Thy Will or thwart Thy Purpose.*
—The Báb

1 Magnified be the majesty of Thine all-encompassing
greatness, and the energizing influence of Thy will!
—Bahá'u'lláh

2 All the wondrous works ye behold in this world
have been manifested through the operation of His
supreme and most exalted Will, His wondrous and
inflexible Purpose.
—Bahá'u'lláh

3 Verily I say, whatever is sent down from the heaven of the Will of God is the means for the establishment of order in the world and the instrument for promoting unity and fellowship among its peoples.

—Bahá'u'lláh

4 O God, my God!
Thou beholdest me circling round Thy Will with mine eyes turned towards the horizon of Thy bounty, eagerly awaiting the revelation of the effulgent splendors of the sun of Thy favors. I beg of Thee, O Beloved of every understanding heart and the Desire of such as have near access unto Thee, to grant that Thy loved ones may become wholly detached from their own inclinations, holding fast unto that which pleaseth Thee. Attire them, O Lord, with the robe of righteousness and illumine them with the splendors of the light of detachment. Summon then to their assistance the hosts of wisdom and utterance that they may exalt Thy Word amongst Thy creatures and proclaim Thy Cause amidst Thy servants.

Verily, potent art Thou to do what Thou willest, and within Thy grasp lie the reins of all affairs. No God is there but Thee, the Mighty, the Ever-Forgiving.

—Bahá'u'lláh

5 Make known . . . Thy station, O my God, unto Thy servants, that they may be made aware that the excellence of all things is dependent upon Thy bidding

and Thy word, and the virtue of every act is conditioned by Thy leave and the good-pleasure of Thy will, and may recognize that the reins of men's doings are within the grasp of Thine acceptance and Thy commandment.

—Bahá'u'lláh

6 Be thou patient and quiet thyself.
    The things thou desirest can last but an hour. As to me, however, I quaff continually in the path of God the cup of His decree, and wish not that the ruling of His will should cease to operate, or that the woes I suffer for the sake of my Lord, the Most Exalted, the All-Glorious, should be ended.

Seek thou my wish and forsake thine own.

—Bahá'u'lláh

7 I have no will of mine own, O my Lord, and my Master and my Ruler, before the indications of Thy will, and can have no purpose in the face of the revelation of Thy purpose. I swear by Thy glory! I wish only what Thou wishest, and cherish only what Thou cherishest. What I have chosen for myself is what Thou hast Thyself chosen for me, O Thou the Possessor of my soul!

—Bahá'u'lláh

8 Aid me, O my Lord, to surrender myself wholly to Thy Will, and to arise and serve Thee . . .

—Bahá'u'lláh

9 I give praise to Thee, O my God, that the fragrance of Thy loving-kindness hath enraptured me, and the gentle winds of Thy mercy have inclined me in the direction of Thy bountiful favors. Make me to quaff, O my Lord, from the fingers of Thy bounteousness the living waters which have enabled every one that hath partaken of them to rid himself of all attachment to any one save Thee, and to soar into the atmosphere of detachment from all Thy creatures, and to fix his gaze upon Thy loving providence and Thy manifold gifts.

Make me ready, in all circumstances, O my Lord, to serve Thee and to set myself towards the adored sanctuary of Thy Revelation and of Thy Beauty. If it be Thy pleasure, make me to grow as a tender herb in the meadows of Thy grace, that the gentle winds of Thy will may stir me up and bend me into conformity with Thy pleasure, in such wise that my movement and my stillness may be wholly directed by Thee.

—Bahá'u'lláh

10 Were any man to ponder in his heart that which the Pen of the Most High hath revealed and to taste of its sweetness, he would, of a certainty, find himself emptied and delivered from his own desires, and utterly subservient to the Will of the Almighty. Happy is the man that hath attained so high a station, and hath not deprived himself of so bountiful a grace.

—Bahá'u'lláh

11 O thou who hast fixed thy gaze upon the Dawning-Place of the Cause of God!

Know thou for a certainty that the Will of God is not limited by the standards of the people, and God doth not tread in their ways. Rather is it incumbent upon everyone to firmly adhere to God's straight Path. Were He to pronounce the right to be the left or the south to be the north, He speaketh the truth and there is no doubt of it. Verily He is to be praised in His acts and to be obeyed in His behests.

He hath no associate in His judgment nor any helper in His sovereignty. He doeth whatsoever He willeth and ordaineth whatsoever He pleaseth.

Know thou moreover that all else besides Him have been created through the potency of a word from His presence, while of themselves they have no motion nor stillness, except at His bidding and by His leave.

—Bahá'u'lláh

12 How can he who is but a creation of Thy will claim to know what is with Thee, or to conceive Thy nature?

—Bahá'u'lláh

13 Be ye guided by wisdom in all your doings, and cleave ye tenaciously unto it. Please God ye may all be strengthened to carry out that which is the Will of God, and may be graciously assisted to appreciate the rank conferred upon such of His loved ones as have arisen to serve Him and magnify His name. Upon them be the glory of God, the glory of all that is in the heavens and all that is on the earth, and the glory of the inmates of the most exalted Paradise, the heaven of heavens.

—Bahá'u'lláh

14 Thou art the King of everlasting days and the supreme Ruler. Thy might is potent over all things and all created things exist by Thy Will.

—The Báb

15 Praised and glorified art Thou, O God!
Grant that the day of attaining Thy holy presence may be fast approaching. Cheer our hearts through the potency of Thy love and good-pleasure and bestow upon us steadfastness that we may willingly submit to Thy Will and Thy Decree.

Verily Thy knowledge embraceth all the things Thou hast created or wilt create and Thy celestial might transcendeth whatsoever Thou hast called or wilt call into being. There is none to be worshipped but Thee, there is none to be desired except Thee, there is none to be adored besides Thee and there is naught to be loved save Thy good-pleasure.

Verily Thou art the supreme Ruler, the Sovereign Truth, the Help in Peril, the Self-Subsisting.

—The Báb

16 The gift of God to this enlightened age is the knowledge of the oneness of mankind and of the fundamental oneness of religion. War shall cease between nations, and by the will of God the Most Great Peace shall come; the world will be seen as a new world, and all men will live as brothers.

—'Abdu'l-Bahá

17 Let nothing grieve thee, and be thou angered at none. It behoveth thee to be content with the Will of God, and a true and loving and trusted friend to all the peoples of the earth, without any exceptions whatever. This is the quality of the sincere, the way of the saints, the emblem of those who believe in the unity of God, and the raiment of the people of Bahá.

—'Abdu'l-Bahá

18 Baha'u'llah has drawn the circle of unity, He has made a design for the uniting of all the peoples, and for the gathering of them all under the shelter of the tent of universal unity. This is the work of the Divine Bounty, and we must all strive with heart and soul until we have the reality of unity in our midst, and as we work, so will strength be given unto us.

Leave all thought of self, and strive only to be obedient and submissive to the Will of God. In this way only shall we become citizens of the Kingdom of God, and attain unto life everlasting.

—'Abdu'l-Bahá

19 . . . when faced with the irrevocable decree of the Almighty, the vesture that best befits us in this world is the vesture of patience and submission, and the most meritorious of all deeds is to commit our affairs into His hands and to surrender ourselves to His Will.

—The Greatest Holy Leaf

O thou who hast surrendered thy will to God!

By self-surrender and perpetual union with God is meant that men should merge their will wholly in the Will of God, and regard their desires as utter nothingness beside His Purpose. Whatsoever the Creator commandeth His creatures to observe, the same must they diligently, and with the utmost joy and eagerness, arise and fulfill. They should in no wise allow their fancy to obscure their judgment, neither should they regard their own imaginings as the voice of the Eternal.

In the Prayer of Fasting We have revealed: "Should Thy Will decree that out of Thy mouth these words proceed and be addressed unto them, 'Observe, for My Beauty's sake, the fast, O people, and set no limit to its duration,' I swear by the majesty of Thy glory, that every one of them will faithfully observe it, will abstain from whatsoever will violate Thy law, and will continue to do so until they yield up their souls unto Thee." In this consisteth the complete surrender of one's will to the Will of God. Meditate on this, that thou mayest drink in the waters of everlasting life which flow through the words of the Lord of all mankind, and mayest testify that the one true God hath ever been immeasurably exalted above His creatures. He, verily, is the Incomparable, the Ever-Abiding, the Omniscient, the All-Wise. The station of absolute self-surrender transcendeth, and will ever remain exalted above, every other station.

It behoveth thee to consecrate thyself to the Will of God. Whatsoever hath been revealed in His Tablets is but a reflection of His Will. So complete must be thy consecration, that every trace of worldly desire will be washed from thine heart. This is the meaning of true unity.

—Bahá'u'lláh

Knowledge

'Ilm

The beginning of all things is the knowledge of God . . .
—Bahá'u'lláh

1 Verily, He Whose knowledge nothing escapeth hath appeared. He Who hath caused the countenance of divine knowledge to be wreathed in smiles is come.

—Bahá'u'lláh

2 By God! The Daystar of Knowledge hath shone forth above the horizon of certitude.

—Bahá'u'lláh

3 How plenteous, O my God, is the stream of Thy knowledge!

—Bahá'u'lláh

4 Verily, if He wished He could make the rays of the sun manifest from an atom, and the waves of the sea from a drop. He hath power, as He hath set forth in detail: the knowledge of what was and what will be, out of a point.

—Bahá'u'lláh

5 The door of the knowledge of the Ancient of Days being thus closed in the face of all beings, the Source of infinite grace . . . hath caused those luminous Gems of Holiness to appear out of the realm of the spirit, in the noble form of the human temple, and be made manifest unto all men, that they may impart unto the world the mysteries of the unchangeable Being, and tell of the subtleties of His imperishable Essence.

These sanctified Mirrors, these Day-springs of ancient glory are one and all the Exponents on earth of Him Who is the central Orb of the universe, its Essence and ultimate Purpose. From Him proceed their knowledge and power; from Him is derived their sovereignty. The beauty of their countenance is but a reflection of His image, and their revelation a sign of His deathless glory.

They are the Treasuries of divine knowledge, and the Repositories of celestial wisdom. Through them is transmitted a grace that is infinite, and by them is revealed the light that can never fade.

—Bahá'u'lláh

6 Glorified art Thou, O Lord my God!
I give Thee thanks inasmuch as Thou hast called me into being in Thy days, and infused into me Thy love and Thy knowledge. I beseech Thee, by Thy name whereby the goodly pearls of Thy wisdom and Thine utterance were brought forth out of the treasuries of the hearts of such of Thy servants as are nigh unto Thee, and through which the Day-Star of Thy name, the Compassionate, hath shed its radiance upon all that are in Thy heaven and on Thy earth, to supply me, by Thy grace and bounty, with Thy wondrous and hidden bounties.

—Bahá'u'lláh

7 Brighten our hearts, O my Lord, with the splendor of Thy knowledge, and illumine our sight with the light of such eyes as are fixed upon the horizon of Thy grace and the Day-Spring of Thy glory.

—Bahá'u'lláh

8 O my brother!
When a true seeker determineth to take the step of search in the path leading to the knowledge of the Ancient of Days, he must, before all else, cleanse and purify his heart, which is the seat of the revelation of the inner mysteries of God, from the obscuring dust of all acquired knowledge, and the allusions of the embodiments of satanic fancy. He must purge his breast, which

is the sanctuary of the abiding love of the Beloved, of every defilement, and sanctify his soul from all that pertaineth to water and clay, from all shadowy and ephemeral attachments. He must so cleanse his heart that no remnant of either love or hate may linger therein, lest that love blindly incline him to error, or that hate repel him away from the truth.

—Bahá'u'lláh

9 . . . man can never hope to attain unto the knowledge of the All-Glorious, can never quaff from the stream of divine knowledge and wisdom, can never enter the abode of immortality, nor partake of the cup of divine nearness and favor, unless and until he ceases to regard the words and deeds of mortal men as a standard for the true understanding and recognition of God and His Prophets.

—Bahá'u'lláh

10 Knowledge is as wings to man's life, and a ladder for his ascent. Its acquisition is incumbent upon everyone. The knowledge of such sciences, however, should be acquired as can profit the peoples of the earth, and not those which begin with words and end with words.

—Bahá'u'lláh

11 Know thou that he is truly learned who hath acknowledged My Revelation, and drunk from the Ocean of My knowledge, and soared in the atmosphere of My love, and cast away all else besides Me, and taken firm hold on that which hath been sent down from the Kingdom of My wondrous utterance.

—Bahá'u'lláh

12 The understanding of His words and the comprehension of the utterances of the Birds of Heaven are in no wise dependent upon human learning. They depend solely upon purity of heart, chastity of soul, and freedom of spirit. This is evidenced by those who, today, though without a single letter of the accepted standards of learning, are occupying the loftiest seats of knowledge; and the garden of their hearts is adorned, through the showers of divine grace, with the roses of wisdom and the tulips of understanding.

Well is it with the sincere in heart for their share of the light of a mighty Day!

—Bahá'u'lláh

13 Let not thine ignorance in human learning and thy inability to read or write grieve thine heart. The doors of His manifold grace are within the mighty grasp of the power of the one true God. He hath opened, and will continue to open, them in the face of all them that serve Him.

—Bahá'u'lláh

14 Every created thing in the whole universe is but a door leading into His knowledge . . .

—Bahá'u'lláh

15 Praise be to God!
The door of divine knowledge has been opened by Baha'u'llah, for He has laid the foundation whereby man may become acquainted with the verities of heaven and earth and has bestowed the utmost confirmation in this day. He is our Teacher and Adviser; He is our Seer and the One clement toward us.

He has prepared His gifts and vouchsafed His bounties, revealed every admonition and behest, prepared for us the means of eternal glory, breathed upon us the life-quickening breaths of the Holy Spirit, opened before our faces the doors of the paradise of Abhá and caused the lights of the Sun of Truth to shine upon us.

—'Abdu'l-Bahá

16 O Lord, help Thou Thy loved ones to acquire knowledge and the sciences and arts, and to unravel the secrets that are treasured up in the inmost reality of all created things. Make them to hear the hidden truths that are written and embedded in the heart of all that is. Make them to be ensigns of guidance amongst all creatures . . .

—'Abdu'l-Bahá

17 . . . mere knowledge is not sufficient for complete human attainment. The teachings of the Holy Books need a heavenly power and divine potency to carry them out. A house is not built by mere acquaintance with the plans. Money must be forthcoming; volition is necessary to construct it; a carpenter must be employed in its erection. It is not enough to say, "The plan and purpose of this house are very good; I will live in it." There are no walls of protection, there is no roof of shelter in this mere statement; the house must be actually built before we can live in it.

—'Abdu'l-Bahá

18 He who hath knowledge and power will rather seek out the glory of heaven, and spiritual distinction, and the life that dieth not.

—'Abdu'l-Bahá

19 O ye roses in the garden of God's love! O ye bright lamps in the assemblage of His knowledge!

May the soft breathings of God pass over you, may the Glory of God illumine the horizon of your hearts. Ye are the waves of the deep sea of knowledge, ye are the massed armies on the plains of certitude, ye are the stars in the skies of God's compassion, ye are the stones that put the people of perdition to flight, ye are clouds of divine pity over the gardens of life, ye are the abundant grace of God's oneness that is shed upon the essences of all created things.

. . . Ye are the birds that soar upward into the firmament of knowledge, the royal falcons on the wrist of God.

—'Abdu'l-Bahá

From **The Valley of Knowledge**

There was once a lover who had sighed for long years in separation from his beloved, and wasted in the fire of remoteness. From the rule of love, his heart was empty of patience, and his body weary of his spirit; he reckoned life without her as a mockery, and time consumed him away. How many a day he found no rest in longing for her; how many a night the pain of her kept him from sleep; his body was worn to a sigh, his heart's wound had turned him to a cry of sorrow. He had given a thousand lives for one taste of the cup of her presence, but it availed him not. The doctors knew no cure for him, and companions avoided his company; yea, physicians have no medicine for one sick of love, unless the favor of the beloved one deliver him.

At last, the tree of his longing yielded the fruit of despair, and the fire of his hope fell to ashes. Then one night he could live no more, and he went out of his house and made for the marketplace. On a sudden, a watchman followed after him. He broke into a run, with the watchman following; then other watchmen came together, and barred every passage to the weary one. And the wretched one cried from his heart, and ran here and there, and moaned to himself: "Surely this watchman is 'Izrá'íl, my angel of death, following so fast upon me; or he is a tyrant of men, seeking to harm me." His feet carried him on, the one bleeding with the arrow of love, and his heart lamented. Then he came to a garden wall, and with untold pain he scaled it, for it proved very high; and forgetting his life, he threw himself down to the garden.

And there he beheld his beloved with a lamp in her hand, searching for a ring she had lost. When the heart-surrendered lover looked on his ravishing love, he drew a great breath and raised up his hands in prayer, crying: "O God! Give Thou glory to the watchman, and riches and long life. For the watchman was Gabriel, guiding this poor one; or he was Isráfíl, bringing life to this wretched one!" . . .

Now if the lover could have looked ahead, he would have blessed the watchman at the start, and prayed on his behalf, and he would have seen that tyranny as justice; but since the end was veiled to him, he moaned and made his plaint in the beginning. Yet those who journey in the garden land of knowledge, because they see the end in the beginning, see peace in war and friendliness in anger.

—Bahá'u'lláh

Power

Qudrat

How great, how very great, are the revelations of Thy wondrous power in all things!
—Bahá'u'lláh

1 Thou art He Whose power is from everlasting to everlasting. Nothing escapeth Thy knowledge. Thou art, verily, the God of power, the God of glory and wisdom.

Praised be God, the Lord of the worlds!

—Bahá'u'lláh

2 Thou, in truth, art the God of strength and power, Who art meet to answer them that pray Thee. There is no God save Thee, the All-Knowing, the All-Wise.

—Bahá'u'lláh

3 . . . no power can endure save through His power, and there is none other God but He.

—Bahá'u'lláh

4 Magnified be Thy name, O my Lord, for Thou hast enabled me to recognize the Manifestation of Thine own Self, and hast caused me to be assured of the truth of the verses which have descended upon Thee. Empower me, I implore Thee, to cling steadfastly unto whatsoever Thou hast bidden me observe. Help me to guard the pearls of Thy love which, by Thy decree, Thou hast enshrined within my heart. Send down, moreover, every moment of my life, O my God, that which will preserve me from any one but Thee, and will set my feet firm in Thy Cause.

Thou art, verily, the God of glory, the God of power, the God of knowledge and wisdom. No God is there beside Thee, the Great Giver, the All-Bountiful, the Almighty, the Ever-Forgiving.

Praised be God, the All-Glorious, the All-Compelling.

—Bahá'u'lláh

5 I beg of Thee, O my God, by Thy power, and Thy might, and Thy sovereignty, which have embraced all who are in Thy heaven and on Thy earth, to make known unto Thy servants this luminous Way and this

straight Path, that they may acknowledge Thy unity and Thy oneness . . .

—Bahá'u'lláh

6 Glorified art Thou, O Lord my God! I pray Thee, by Him Who is the Day-Spring of Thy signs and the Manifestation of Thy names, and the Treasury of Thine inspiration, and the Repository of Thy wisdom, to send upon Thy loved ones that which will enable them to cleave steadfastly to Thy Cause, and to recognize Thy unity, and to acknowledge Thy oneness, and to bear witness to Thy divinity. Raise them up, O my God, to such heights that they will recognize in all things the tokens of the power of Him Who is the Manifestation of Thy most august and all-glorious Self.

Thou art He, O my Lord, Who doeth what He willeth, and ordaineth what He pleaseth. Every possessor of power is forlorn before the revelations of Thy might, and every fountain of honor becomes abject when confronted by the manifold evidences of Thy great glory.

I beseech Thee, by Thyself and by whatsoever is of Thee, to grant that I may help Thy Cause and speak of Thy praise, and set my heart on the sanctuary of Thy glory, and detach myself from all that pertaineth not unto Thee. No God is there beside Thee, the God of power, the God of glory and wisdom.

—Bahá'u'lláh

7 All the atoms of the earth bear witness, O my Lord, to the greatness of Thy power and of Thy sovereignty; and all the signs of the universe attest the glory of Thy majesty and of Thy might.

—Bahá'u'lláh

8 O Son of Spirit!
The spirit of holiness beareth unto thee the joyful tidings of reunion; wherefore dost thou grieve? The spirit of power confirmeth thee in His cause; why dost thou veil thyself? The light of His countenance doth lead thee; how canst thou go astray?

—Bahá'u'lláh

9 O Son of Spirit!
I created thee rich, why dost thou bring thyself down to poverty? Noble I made thee, wherewith dost thou abase thyself? Out of the essence of knowledge I gave thee being, why seekest thou enlightenment from anyone beside Me? Out of the clay of love I molded thee, how dost thou busy thyself with another? Turn thy sight unto thyself, that thou mayest find Me standing within thee, mighty, powerful and self-subsisting.

—Bahá'u'lláh

10 Our limbs, our members, O my Lord, bear witness to Thy unity and oneness. Send down upon us Thy strength and power, that we may become steadfast in Thy Faith and may aid Thee among Thy servants.

—Bahá'u'lláh

11 Hold Thou me with the hands of Thy power, and grant that I may be so carried away by the sweet melodies of the Dove of Thy oneness, that I will cease to regard in all creation any face except Thy face, O Thou the Goal of my desire, and will recognize in the visible world naught else save the evidences of Thy might, O Thou Who art the God of mercy!

—Bahá'u'lláh

12 One righteous act is endowed with a potency that can so elevate the dust as to cause it to pass beyond the heaven of heavens. It can tear every bond asunder, and hath the power to restore the force that hath spent itself and vanished. . . .

Be pure, O people of God, be pure; be righteous, be righteous.

—Bahá'u'lláh

13 Lauded and glorified art Thou, O Lord my God! Thou art supreme over the realm of being and Thy power pervadeth all created things.

—The Báb

14 O Thou Who art the Lord of grace abounding!
Let Thy celestial aid surround those who love
Thee and bestow upon us the gifts and the bounties
Thou dost possess. Be Thou sufficient unto us of all
things, forgive our sins and have mercy upon us. Thou
art Our Lord and the Lord of all created things. No one
else do we invoke but Thee and naught do we beseech
but Thy favors.

Thou art the Lord of bounty and grace, invincible in
Thy power and the most skillful in Thy designs. No God
is there but Thee, the All-Possessing, the Most Exalted.

—The Báb

15 Say, the power of God is in the hearts of those who
believe in the unity of God and bear witness that
no God is there but Him . . .

—The Báb

16 Whensoever holy souls, drawing on the powers of
heaven, shall arise with such qualities of the spirit,
and march in unison, rank on rank, every one of those
souls will be even as one thousand, and the surging
waves of that mighty ocean will be even as the battalions
of the Concourse on high. What a blessing that will be . . .

—'Abdu'l-Bahá

17 Do not take into consideration your own aptitudes and capacities, but fix your gaze on the consummate bounty, the divine bestowal and the power of the Holy Spirit — the power that converteth the drop into a sea and the star into a sun.

—'Abdu'l-Bahá

18 Now, through the aid and bounty of God, this power of guidance and this merciful bestowal are found in thee. Arise, therefore, in the utmost Power that thou mayest bestow spirit upon moldering bones, give sight to the blind, balm and freshness to the depressed, and liveliness and grace to the dispirited.

—'Abdu'l-Bahá

19 O Lord! Confirm me with the Holy Spirit, so that I may call in Thy Name amongst the nations, and give the glad tidings of the manifestation of Thy kingdom amongst mankind.

O Lord! I am weak, strengthen me with Thy power and potency. My tongue falters, suffer me to utter Thy commemoration and praise. I am lowly, honor me through admitting me into Thy kingdom. I am remote, cause me to approach the threshold of Thy mercifulness.

O Lord! Make me a brilliant lamp, a shining star and a blessed tree, adorned with fruit, its branches overshadowing all these regions. Verily, Thou art the Mighty, the Powerful and Unconstrained.

—'Abdu'l-Bahá

Know thou of a certainty that Love is the secret of God's holy Dispensation, the manifestation of the All-Merciful, the fountain of spiritual outpourings. Love is heaven's kindly light, the Holy Spirit's eternal breath that vivifieth the human soul. Love is the cause of God's revelation unto man, the vital bond inherent, in accordance with the divine creation, in the realities of things. Love is the one means that ensureth true felicity both in this world and the next. Love is the light that guideth in darkness, the living link that uniteth God with man, that assureth the progress of every illumined soul.

Love is the most great law that ruleth this mighty and heavenly cycle, the unique power that bindeth together the divers elements of this material world, the supreme magnetic force that directeth the movements of the spheres in the celestial realms.

Love revealeth with unfailing and limitless power the mysteries latent in the universe.

—'Abdu'l-Bahá

Speech

Qawl

This is the day in which to speak.
—Bahá'u'lláh

1 He is God, exalted is He, the Lord of wisdom and utterance.

—Bahá'u'lláh

2 He is the One Who speaketh through the power of Truth in the Kingdom of Utterance.

—Bahá'u'lláh

3 Praise be unto God, incomparable in majesty, power and beauty, peerless in glory, might and grandeur; too high is He for human imaginations to comprehend Him or for any peer or equal to be ascribed unto Him.

He hath clearly set forth His straight Path in words and utterances of highest eloquence.

—Bahá'u'lláh

4 I render Thee thanks, O Thou Who hast lighted Thy fire within my soul, and cast the beams of Thy light into my heart, that Thou hast taught Thy servants how to make mention of Thee, and revealed unto them the ways whereby they can supplicate Thee, through Thy most holy and exalted tongue, and Thy most august and precious speech.

—Bahá'u'lláh

5 Thou knowest, O my Lord, that I am but one of Thy servants. I have tasted of the sweetness of Thy speech, and acknowledged Thy unity and Thy singleness, and set my face towards the Source of Thy most excellent names and the Day-Spring of Thy transcendent attributes, and wished to be enabled by Thee to immerse myself beneath the ocean of Thy oneness and to be submerged by the mighty waters of Thy unity.

—Bahá'u'lláh

6 He is a man of insight whose eyes have been illumined with the brightness of Thy face, and who, as soon as Thy call was raised, hath recognized Thee. He is a man of hearing who hath been led to hearken unto

Thy speech, and to draw nigh unto the billowing ocean of Thine utterances.

—Bahá'u'lláh

7 Myriads of mystic tongues find utterance in one speech, and myriads of hidden mysteries are revealed in a single melody; yet, alas, there is no ear to hear, nor heart to understand.

—Bahá'u'lláh

8 Say: If it be Our pleasure We shall render the Cause victorious through the power of a single word from Our presence. He is in truth the Omnipotent, the All-Compelling. Should it be God's intention, there would appear out of the forests of celestial might the lion of indomitable strength whose roaring is like unto the peals of thunder reverberating in the mountains.

However, since Our loving providence surpasseth all things, We have ordained that complete victory should be achieved through speech and utterance, that Our servants throughout the earth may thereby become the recipients of divine good. This is but a token of God's bounty vouchsafed unto them. Verily thy Lord is the All-Sufficing, the Most Exalted.

—Bahá'u'lláh

9 Be fair in thy judgment, and guarded in thy speech.

—Bahá'u'lláh

10   Verily I say, the tongue is for mentioning what is good, defile it not with unseemly talk. God hath forgiven what is past. Henceforward everyone should utter that which is meet and seemly, and should refrain from slander, abuse and whatever causeth sadness in men.

—Bahá'u'lláh

11   Open, O people, the city of the human heart with the key of your utterance. Thus have We, according to a pre-ordained measure, prescribed unto you your duty.

—Bahá'u'lláh

12   The sanctified souls should ponder and meditate in their hearts regarding the methods of teaching. From the texts of the wondrous, heavenly Scriptures they should memorize phrases and passages bearing on various instances, so that in the course of their speech they may recite divine verses whenever the occasion demandeth it, inasmuch as these holy verses are the most potent elixir, the greatest and mightiest talisman. So potent is their influence that the hearer will have no cause for vacillation. I swear by My life! This Revelation is endowed with such a power that it will act as the lodestone for all nations and kindreds of the earth.

—Bahá'u'lláh

13 . . . Good News! Good News! For Everlasting Life is here!

O Ye that sleep, Awake!
O Ye heedless ones, Learn wisdom!
O Blind, receive your sight!
O Deaf, Hear!
O Dumb, Speak!
O Dead, Arise!
Be Happy!
Be Happy!
Be full of Joy!

—'Abdu'l-Bahá

14 . . . he should speak with the utmost kindliness, lowliness and humility, for such speech exerteth influence and educateth the souls.

—'Abdu'l-Bahá

15 It is at such times that the friends of God avail themselves of the occasion, seize the opportunity, rush forth and win the prize. If their task is to be confined to good conduct and advice, nothing will be accomplished. They must speak out, expound the proofs, set forth clear arguments, draw irrefutable conclusions establishing the truth of the manifestation of the Sun of Reality.

—'Abdu'l-Bahá

16 Follow thou the way of thy Lord, and say not that which the ears cannot bear to hear, for such speech is like luscious food given to small children. However palatable, rare and rich the food may be, it cannot be assimilated by the digestive organs of a suckling child. Therefore unto every one who hath a right, let his settled measure be given.

"Not everything that a man knoweth can be disclosed, nor can everything that he can disclose be regarded as timely, nor can every timely utterance be considered as suited to the capacity of those who hear it." Such is the consummate wisdom to be observed in thy pursuits.

—'Abdu'l-Bahá

17 Praise be to God! The standard of liberty is held aloft in this land [America].

You enjoy political liberty; you enjoy liberty of thought and speech, religious liberty, racial and personal liberty. Surely this is worthy of appreciation and thanksgiving.

—'Abdu'l-Bahá

18 . . . in democracy, because thought and speech are not restricted, the greatest progress is witnessed. It is likewise true in the world of religion. When freedom of conscience, liberty of thought and right of speech prevail—that is to say, when every man according to his

own idealization may give expression to his beliefs—development and growth are inevitable.

—'Abdu'l-Bahá

19 Ye have written as to the meetings of the friends, and how filled they are with peace and joy. Of course this is so; for wherever the spiritually minded are gathered together, there in His beauty reigneth Bahá'u'lláh. Thus it is certain that such reunions will yield boundless happiness and peace.

Today it behoveth one and all to forgo the mention of all else, and to disregard all things. Let their speaking, let their inner state be summed up thus: "Keep all my words of prayer and praise confined to one refrain; make all my life but servitude to Thee."

That is, let them concentrate all their thoughts, all their words, on teaching the Cause of God and spreading the Faith of God, and inspiring all to characterize themselves with the characteristics of God; on loving mankind; on being pure and holy in all things, and spotless in their public and private life; on being upright and detached, and fervent, and afire.

—'Abdu'l-Bahá

Every word is endowed with a spirit, therefore the speaker or expounder should carefully deliver his words at the appropriate time and place, for the impression which each word maketh is clearly evident and perceptible.

The Great Being saith: One word may be likened unto fire, another unto light, and the influence which both exert is manifest in the world. Therefore an enlightened man of wisdom should primarily speak with words as mild as milk, that the children of men may be nurtured and edified thereby and may attain the ultimate goal of human existence which is the station of true understanding and nobility.

—Bahá'u'lláh

Questions

Masá'il

Dost thou reckon thyself only a puny form when within thee the universe is folded?
—Bahá'u'lláh, quoting the Imám 'Alí

1 Know ye from what heights your Lord, the All-Glorious, is calling? Think ye that ye have recognized the Pen wherewith your Lord, the Lord of all names, commandeth you? Nay, by My life! Did ye but know it, ye would renounce the world, and would hasten with your whole hearts to the presence of the Well-Beloved.

—Bahá'u'lláh

2 I give thanks to Thee, O my God, that Thou hast suffered me to remember Thee. What else but remembrance of Thee can give delight to my soul or gladness to my heart?

—Bahá'u'lláh

3 Whither can a lover go but to the land of his beloved? and what seeker findeth rest away from his heart's desire? To the true lover reunion is life, and separation is death.

—Bahá'u'lláh

4 Glory to Thee, O my God!
But for the tribulations which are sustained in Thy path, how could Thy true lovers be recognized; and were it not for the trials which are borne for love of Thee, how could the station of such as yearn for Thee be revealed?

—Bahá'u'lláh

5 Cause me, O my Lord, to be reckoned among them who have been so stirred up by the sweet savors that have been wafted in Thy days that they have laid down their lives for Thee and hastened to the scene of their death in their longing to gaze on Thy beauty and in their yearning to attain Thy presence. And were any one to say unto them on their way, "Whither go ye?" they would say, "Unto God, the All-Possessing, the Help in Peril, the Self-Subsisting!"

—Bahá'u'lláh

6 In the Bayán it had been forbidden you to ask Us questions. The Lord hath now relieved you of this prohibition, that ye may be free to ask what you need to

ask, but not such idle questions as those on which the men of former times were wont to dwell. Fear God, and be ye of the righteous! Ask ye that which shall be of profit to you in the Cause of God and His dominion, for the portals of His tender compassion have been opened before all who dwell in heaven and on earth.

—Bahá'u'lláh

7 We noted the questions thou hast asked and will readily answer thee. It behoveth everyone in this Day to ask God that which he desireth, and thy Lord will heed his petition with wondrous and undeniable verses.

—Bahá'u'lláh

8 Even as He hath revealed: "Do men think when they say 'We believe' they shall be let alone and not be put to proof?"

—Bahá'u'lláh

9 Ponder then in thine heart: Matters being such as thou dost witness, and as We also witness, where canst thou flee, and with whom shalt thou take refuge? Unto whom wilt thou turn thy gaze? In what land shalt thou dwell and upon what seat shalt thou abide? In what path shalt thou tread and at what hour wilt thou find repose? What shall become of thee in the end? Where

shalt thou secure the cord of they faith and fasten the tie of thine obedience?

—Bahá'u'lláh

10 Through the movement of Our Pen of glory We have, at the bidding of the omnipotent Ordainer, breathed a new life into every human frame, and instilled into every word a fresh potency. All created things proclaim the evidences of this world-wide regeneration. This is the most great, the most joyful tidings imparted by the Pen of this wronged One to mankind.

Wherefore fear ye, O My well-beloved ones? Who is it that can dismay you? A touch of moisture sufficeth to dissolve the hardened clay out of which this perverse generation is molded. The mere act of your gathering together is enough to scatter the forces of these vain and worthless people. . . .

—Bahá'u'lláh

11 Is there any Remover of difficulties save God? Say: Praised be God! He is God! All are His servants, and all abide by His bidding!

—The Báb

12 Is there any doubt concerning God? He hath created you and all things. The Lord of all worlds is He.

—The Báb

13 O ye friends of God! Do ye know in what cycle ye are created and in what age ye exist? This is the age of the Blessed Perfection and this is the time of the Greatest Name! This is the century of the Manifestation, the age of the Sun of the horizons and the beautiful springtime of the Eternal One!

—'Abdu'l-Bahá

14 Do you appreciate the Day in which you live? This is the century of the Blessed Perfection! This is the cycle of the light of His beauty! This is the consummate day of all the Prophets!

—'Abdu'l-Bahá

15 If we are not happy and joyous at this season, for what other season shall we wait and for what other time shall we look?

Boundless treasure is in the hand of the King of Kings! Lift the hem of thy garment to receive it.

This is the time for growing; the season for joyous gathering! Take the cup of the Testament in thy hand, leap and dance with ecstasy in the triumphal procession of the Covenant!

—'Abdu'l-Bahá

16 Turn your faces to the Sun of Reality. . . . Find the answer to your questions in your heart.

—'Abdu'l-Bahá

17 . . . Is there any deed in the world that would be nobler than service to the common good? Is there any greater blessing conceivable for a man, than that he should become the cause of the education, the development, the prosperity and honor of his fellow-creatures? No, by the Lord God! The highest righteousness of all is for blessed souls to take hold of the hands of the helpless and deliver them out of their ignorance and abasement and poverty, and with pure motives, and only for the sake of God, to arise and energetically devote themselves to the service of the masses, forgetting their own worldly advantage and working only to serve the general good.

—'Abdu'l-Bahá

18 What is real unity?

—'Abdu'l-Bahá

19 Is there a greater blessing than this? Freedom! Liberty! Security! These are the great bestowals of God. Therefore, praise ye God!

—'Abdu'l-Bahá

The Fire Tablet

In the Name of God, the Most Ancient, the Most Great.

*I*ndeed the hearts of the sincere are consumed in the fire of separation: Where is the gleaming of the light of Thy Countenance, O Beloved of the worlds?

Those who are near unto Thee have been abandoned in the darkness of desolation: Where is the shining of the morn of Thy reunion, O Desire of the worlds?

The bodies of Thy chosen ones lie quivering on distant sands: Where is the ocean of Thy presence, O Enchanter of the worlds?

Longing hands are uplifted to the heaven of Thy grace and generosity: Where are the rains of Thy bestowal, O Answerer of the worlds?

The infidels have arisen in tyranny on every hand: Where is the compelling power of Thine ordaining pen, O Conqueror of the worlds?

The barking of dogs is loud on every side: Where is the lion of the forest of Thy might, O Chastiser of the worlds?

Coldness hath gripped all mankind: Where is the warmth of Thy love, O Fire of the worlds?

Calamity hath reached its height: Where are the signs of Thy succor, O Salvation of the worlds?

Darkness hath enveloped most of the peoples: Where is the brightness of Thy splendor, O Radiance of the worlds?

The necks of men are stretched out in malice: Where are the swords of Thy vengeance, O Destroyer of the worlds?

Abasement hath reached its lowest depth: Where are the emblems of Thy glory, O Glory of the worlds?

Sorrows have afflicted the Revealer of Thy Name, the All-Merciful: Where is the joy of the Dayspring of Thy Revelation, O Delight of the worlds?

Anguish hath befallen all the peoples of the earth: Where are the ensigns of Thy gladness, O Joy of the worlds?

Thou seest the Dawning Place of Thy signs veiled by evil suggestions: Where are the fingers of Thy might, O Power of the worlds?

Sore thirst hath overcome all men: Where is the river of Thy bounty, O Mercy of the worlds?

Greed hath made captive all mankind: Where are the embodiments of detachment, O Lord of the worlds?

Thou seest this Wronged One lonely in exile: Where are the hosts of the heaven of Thy Command, O Sovereign of the worlds?

I have been forsaken in a foreign land: Where are the emblems of Thy faithfulness, O Trust of the worlds?

The agonies of death have laid hold on all men: Where is the surging of Thine ocean of eternal life, O Life of the worlds?

The whisperings of Satan have been breathed to every creature: Where is the meteor of Thy fire, O Light of the worlds?

The drunkenness of passion hath perverted most of mankind: Where are the daysprings of purity, O Desire of the worlds?

Thou seest this Wronged One veiled in tyranny among the Syrians: Where is the radiance of Thy dawning light, O Light of the worlds?

Thou seest Me forbidden to speak forth: Then from where will spring Thy melodies, O Nightingale of the worlds?

Most of the people are enwrapped in fancy and idle imaginings: Where are the exponents of Thy certitude, O Assurance of the worlds?

Bahá is drowning in a sea of tribulation: Where is the Ark of Thy salvation, O Savior of the worlds?

Thou seest the Dayspring of Thine utterance in the darkness of creation: Where is the sun of the heaven of Thy grace, O Lightgiver of the worlds?

The lamps of truth and purity, of loyalty and honor, have been put out: Where are the signs of Thine avenging wrath, O Mover of the worlds?

Canst Thou see any who have championed Thy Self, or who ponder on what hath befallen Him in the pathway of Thy love? Now doth My pen halt, O Beloved of the worlds.

The branches of the Divine Lote-Tree lie broken by the onrushing gales of destiny: Where are the banners of Thy succor, O Champion of the worlds?

This Face is hidden in the dust of slander: Where are the breezes of Thy compassion, O Mercy of the worlds?

The robe of sanctity is sullied by the people of deceit: Where is the vesture of Thy holiness, O Adorner of the worlds?

The sea of grace is stilled for what the hands of men have wrought: Where are the waves of Thy bounty, O Desire of the worlds?

The door leading to the Divine Presence is locked through the tyranny of Thy foes: Where is the key of Thy bestowal, O Unlocker of the worlds?

The leaves are yellowed by the poisoning winds of sedition: Where is the downpour of the clouds of Thy bounty, O Giver of the worlds?

The universe is darkened with the dust of sin: Where are the breezes of Thy forgiveness, O Forgiver of the worlds?

This Youth is lonely in a desolate land: Where is the rain of Thy heavenly grace, O Bestower of the worlds?

O Supreme Pen, We have heard Thy most sweet call in the eternal realm: Give Thou ear unto what the Tongue of Grandeur uttereth, O Wronged One of the worlds!

Were it not for the cold, how would the heat of Thy words prevail, O Expounder of the worlds? Were it not for calamity, how would the sun of Thy patience shine, O Light of the worlds?

Lament not because of the wicked. Thou wert created to bear and endure, O Patience of the worlds. How sweet was Thy dawning on the horizon of the Covenant among the stirrers of sedition, and Thy yearning after God, O Love of the worlds.

By Thee the banner of independence was planted on the highest peaks, and the sea of bounty surged, O Rapture of the worlds.

By Thine aloneness the Sun of Oneness shone, and by Thy banishment the land of Unity was adorned. Be patient, O Thou Exile of the worlds.

We have made abasement the garment of glory, and affliction the adornment of Thy temple, O Pride of the worlds. Thou seest the hearts are filled with hate, and to overlook is Thine, O Thou Concealer of the sins of the worlds.

When the swords flash, go forward! When the shafts fly, press onward! O Thou Sacrifice of the worlds.

Dost Thou wail, or shall I wail? Rather shall I weep at the fewness of Thy champions, O Thou Who hast caused the wailing of the worlds.

Verily, I have heard Thy call, O All-Glorious Beloved; and now is the face of Bahá flaming with the heat of tribulation and with the fire of Thy shining word, and He hath risen up in faithfulness at the place of sacrifice, looking toward Thy pleasure, O Ordainer of the worlds.

O 'Alí-Akbar, thank thy Lord for this Tablet whence thou canst breathe the fragrances of My meekness, and know what hath beset Us in the path of God, the Adored of all the worlds. Should all the servants read and ponder this, there shall be kindled in their veins a fire that shall set aflame the worlds.

—Bahá'u'lláh

Honor

Sharaf

*. . . the honor of the human kingdom is the attainment of spiritual
happiness in the human world, the acquisition of
the knowledge and love of God.*
—'Abdu'l-Bahá

1 All laud and honor to Thee, O my God!
—Bahá'u'lláh

2 All praise to the unity of God, and all honor to
Him, the sovereign Lord, the incomparable and all-
glorious Ruler of the universe, Who, out of utter nothingness, hath created the reality of all things . . .
—Bahá'u'lláh

3 All praise, O my God, be to Thee Who art the Source of all glory and majesty, of greatness and honor, of sovereignty and dominion, of loftiness and grace, of awe and power. Whomsoever Thou willest Thou causest to draw nigh unto the Most Great Ocean, and on whomsoever Thou desirest Thou conferrest the honor of recognizing Thy Most Ancient Name. Of all who are in heaven and on earth, none can withstand the operation of Thy sovereign Will.

From all eternity Thou didst rule the entire creation, and Thou wilt continue for evermore to exercise Thy dominion over all created things. There is none other God but Thee, the Almighty, the Most Exalted, the All-Powerful, the All-Wise.

Illumine, O Lord, the faces of Thy servants, that they may behold Thee; and cleanse their hearts that they may turn unto the court of Thy heavenly favors, and recognize Him Who is the Manifestation of Thy Self and the Day-Spring of Thine Essence.

Verily, Thou art the Lord of all worlds. There is no God but Thee, the Unconstrained, the All-Subduing.

—Bahá'u'lláh

4 How great the blessedness that awaiteth him that hath attained the honor of serving the Almighty! By My life! No act, however great, can compare with it, except such deeds as have been ordained by God, the All-Powerful, the Most Mighty.

—Bahá'u'lláh

5 Ere long the world and all that is therein shall be as a thing forgotten, and all honor shall belong to the loved ones of thy Lord, the All-Glorious, the Most Bountiful.

—Bahá'u'lláh

6 Behold, how the divers peoples and kindreds of the earth have been waiting for the coming of the Promised One. No sooner had He, Who is the Sun of Truth, been made manifest, than, lo, all turned away from Him, except them whom God was pleased to guide. We dare not, in this Day, lift the veil that concealeth the exalted station which every true believer can attain, for the joy which such a revelation must provoke might well cause a few to faint away and die. . . .

Whoso hath searched the depths of the oceans that lie hid within these exalted words, and fathomed their import, can be said to have discovered a glimmer of the unspeakable glory with which this mighty, this sublime, and most holy Revelation hath been endowed. From the excellence of so great a Revelation the honor with which its faithful followers must needs be invested can be well imagined.

By the righteousness of the one true God! The very breath of these souls is in itself richer than all the treasures of the earth.

—Bahá'u'lláh

7 Blessed is the man that hath acknowledged his belief in God and in His signs, and recognized that "He shall not be asked of His doings." . . .

Whoso hath not recognized this sublime and fundamental verity, and hath failed to attain this most exalted station, the winds of doubt will agitate him, and the sayings of the infidels will distract his soul. He that hath acknowledged this principle will be endowed with the most perfect constancy.

All honor to this all-glorious station, the remembrance of which adorneth every exalted Tablet. Such is the teaching which God bestoweth on you, a teaching that will deliver you from all manner of doubt and perplexity, and enable you to attain unto salvation in both this world and in the next.

He, verily, is the Ever-Forgiving, the Most Bountiful.

—Bahá'u'lláh

8 Pay thou no heed to the humiliation to which the loved ones of God have in this Day been subjected. This humiliation is the pride and glory of all temporal honor and worldly elevation. What greater honor can be imagined than the honor conferred by the Tongue of the Ancient of Days when He calleth to remembrance His loved ones . . .? The day is approaching when the intervening clouds will have been completely dissipated, when the light of the words, "All honor belongeth unto God and unto them that love Him," will have appeared,

as manifest as the sun, above the horizon of the Will of the Almighty.

All men, be they high or low, have sought and are still seeking so great an honor. All, however, have, as soon as the Sun of Truth shed its radiance upon the world, been deprived of its benefits, and have been shut out as by a veil from its glory, except them that have clung to the cord of the unfailing providence of the one true God, and have with complete detachment from all else but Him turned their faces towards His holy court.

Render thanks unto Him Who is the Desire of all worlds for having invested thee with such high honor.

—Bahá'u'lláh

9 All praise be unto Thee, O Thou besides Whom there is none other God. Graciously enable me to ascend unto Thee, to be granted the honor of dwelling in Thy nearness and to have communion with Thee alone.

—The Báb

10 The honor allotted to man is the acquisition of the supreme virtues of the human world. This is his real happiness and felicity.

—'Abdu'l-Bahá

11 The honor of man is through the attainment of the knowledge of God; his happiness is from the love of God; his joy is in the glad tidings of God; his greatness is dependent upon his servitude to God. The highest development of man is his entrance into the divine Kingdom, and the outcome of this human existence is the nucleus and essence of eternal life.

—'Abdu'l-Bahá

12 Then it is clear that the honor and exaltation of man must be something more than material riches. Material comforts are only a branch, but the root of the exaltation of man is the good attributes and virtues which are the adornments of his reality. These are the divine appearances, the heavenly bounties, the sublime emotions, the love and knowledge of God; universal wisdom, intellectual perception, scientific discoveries, justice, equity, truthfulness, benevolence, natural courage and innate fortitude; the respect for rights and the keeping of agreements and covenants; rectitude in all circumstances; serving the truth under all conditions; the sacrifice of one's life for the good of all people; kindness and esteem for all nations; obedience to the teachings of God; service in the Divine Kingdom; the guidance of the people, and the education of the nations and races. This is the prosperity of the human world! This is the exaltation of man in the world! This is eternal life and heavenly honor!

—'Abdu'l-Bahá

13 . . . knowledge is the most glorious gift of man and the most noble of human perfections. . . . For knowledge is light, life, felicity, perfection, beauty and the means of approaching the Threshold of Unity. It is the honor and glory of the world of humanity, and the greatest bounty of God.

—'Abdu'l-Bahá

14 It is certain that man's highest distinction is to be lowly before and obedient to his God; that his greatest glory, his most exalted rank and honor, depend on his close observance of the Divine commands and prohibitions. Religion is the light of the world, and the progress, achievement, and happiness of man result from obedience to the laws set down in the holy Books.

—'Abdu'l-Bahá

15 . . . man's supreme honor and real happiness lie in self-respect, in high resolves and noble purposes, in integrity and moral quality, in immaculacy of mind.

—'Abdu'l-Bahá

16 It is clearly evident that while man possesses powers in common with the animal, he is distinguished from the animal by intellectual attainment, spiritual perception, the acquisition of virtues, capacity to receive the bestowals of Divinity, lordly bounty and emanations of heavenly mercy. This is the adornment of man, his honor and sublimity. Humanity must strive toward this supreme station.

—'Abdu'l-Bahá

17 Science ever tends to the illumination of the world of humanity. It is the cause of eternal honor to man, and its sovereignty is far greater than the sovereignty of kings. The dominion of kings has an ending; the king himself may be dethroned; but the sovereignty of science is everlasting and without end.

—'Abdu'l-Bahá

18 Religion confers upon man eternal life and guides his footsteps in the world of morality. It opens the doors of unending happiness and bestows everlasting honor upon the human kingdom.

—'Abdu'l-Bahá

19 O Thou compassionate Lord, Thou Who art generous and able!

We are servants of Thine sheltered beneath Thy providence. Cast Thy glance of favor upon us. Give light to our eyes, hearing to our ears, and understanding and love to our hearts. Render our souls joyous and happy through Thy glad tidings.

O Lord! Point out to us the pathway of Thy kingdom and resuscitate all of us through the breaths of the Holy

Spirit. Bestow upon us life everlasting and confer upon us never-ending honor. Unify mankind and illumine the world of humanity. May we all follow Thy pathway, long for Thy good pleasure and seek the mysteries of Thy kingdom.

O God! Unite us and connect our hearts with Thy indissoluble bond.

Verily, Thou art the Giver, Thou art the Kind One and Thou art the Almighty.

—'Abdu'l-Bahá

The man who thinks only of himself and is thoughtless of others is undoubtedly inferior to the animal because the animal is not possessed of the reasoning faculty. The animal is excused; but in man there is reason, the faculty of justice, the faculty of mercifulness. Possessing all these faculties he must not leave them unused. He who is so hard-hearted as to think only of his own comfort, such an one will not be called man.

Man is he who forgets his own interests for the sake of others. His own comfort he forfeits for the well-being of all. Nay, rather, his own life must he be willing to forfeit for the life of mankind.

Such a man is the honor of the world of humanity. Such a man is the glory of the world of mankind. Such a man is the one who wins eternal bliss. Such a man is near to the threshold of God. Such a man is the very manifestation of eternal happiness. Otherwise, men are like animals, exhibiting the same proclivities and propensities as the world of animals. What distinction is there? What prerogatives, what perfections? None whatever! Animals are better even—thinking only of themselves and negligent of the needs of others.

Consider how the greatest men in the world—whether among prophets or philosophers—all have forfeited their own comfort, have sacrificed their own pleasure for the well-being of humanity. They have sacrificed their own lives for the body politic. They have sacrificed their own wealth for that of the general welfare. They have forfeited their own honor for the honor of mankind.

Therefore it becomes evident that this is the highest attainment for the world of humanity.

—'Abdu'l-Bahá

Sovereignty

Sultán

Whether ye rejoice or whether ye burst for fury, the heavens are cleft asunder, and God hath come down, invested with radiant sovereignty.
—Bahá'u'lláh

1 Glorified art Thou, O Lord my God! Every man of insight confesseth Thy sovereignty and Thy dominion, and every discerning eye perceiveth the greatness of Thy majesty and the compelling power of Thy might.
—Bahá'u'lláh

2 . . . the Voice of the Ancient of Days, crying to thee from the Kingdom of His all-glorious Name . . . is now proclaiming from the realms above, and within the inmost essence of all created things: "I truly am God, there is none other God but Me. I am He Who, from everlasting, hath been the Source of all sovereignty and power, He Who shall continue, throughout eternity, to exercise His kingship and to extend His protection unto all created things. My proof is the greatness of My might and My sovereignty that embraceth the whole of creation."

—Bahá'u'lláh

3 He, in truth, witnesseth, and perceiveth, and doeth what He pleaseth, through the power of His sovereignty. He, verily, is the Lord of strength, and of might.

—Bahá'u'lláh

4 Verily, We have caused every soul to expire by virtue of Our irresistible and all-subduing sovereignty. We have, then, called into being a new creation, as a token of Our grace unto men.

—Bahá'u'lláh

5 Thou art He to Whose power and to Whose dominion every tongue hath testified, and Whose majesty and Whose sovereignty every understanding heart hath acknowledged. No God is there but Thee, Who hearest and art ready to answer.

—Bahá'u'lláh

6 Know thou that every created thing is a sign of the revelation of God. Each, according to its capacity, is, and will ever remain, a token of the Almighty. Inasmuch as He, the sovereign Lord of all, hath willed to reveal His sovereignty in the kingdom of names and attributes, each and every created thing hath, through the act of the Divine Will, been made a sign of His glory.

—Bahá'u'lláh

7 The hour is approaching when ye will witness the power of the one true God triumphing over all created things and the signs of His sovereignty encompassing all creation.

let it be!

—Bahá'u'lláh

8 You will readily recognize that the terms sovereignty, wealth, life, death, judgment and resurrection, spoken of by the scriptures of old, are not what this generation hath conceived and vainly imagined. Nay, by sovereignty is meant that sovereignty which in every dispensation resideth within, and is exercised by, the person of the Manifestation, the Day-star of Truth. That sovereignty is the spiritual ascendancy which He exerciseth to the fullest degree over all that is in heaven and on earth, and which in due time revealeth itself to the world in direct proportion to its capacity and spiritual receptiveness . . .

—Bahá'u'lláh

9 Raise up, I implore Thee, O my God, as helpers to this Revelation such as shall be counted worthy of Thy Name and of Thy sovereignty . . .

—Bahá'u'lláh

10 O Son of Spirit!
My first counsel is this: Possess a pure, kindly and radiant heart, that thine may be a sovereignty ancient, imperishable and everlasting.

—Bahá'u'lláh

11 O Son of Utterance!
Turn thy face unto Mine and renounce all save Me; for My sovereignty endureth and My dominion perisheth not.

—Bahá'u'lláh

12 O Son of My Handmaid!
Didst thou behold immortal sovereignty, thou wouldst strive to pass from this fleeting world. But to conceal the one from thee and to reveal the other is a mystery which none but the pure in heart can comprehend.

—Bahá'u'lláh

13 Seize ye the chalice of constancy through the power of His Name, quaff then therefrom by virtue of the sovereignty of God, the Powerful, the Omnipotent.

—Bahá'u'lláh

14 Say, take heed lest the overpowering might of the oppressors alarm you. The day is approaching when every emblem of vainglory will have been reduced to nothingness; then shall ye behold the invincible sovereignty of your Lord ruling over all things visible and invisible.

—Bahá'u'lláh

15 O God our Lord! . . .
Thy loving providence hath encompassed all created things in the heavens and on the earth, and Thy forgiveness hath surpassed the whole creation. Thine is sovereignty; in Thy hand are the Kingdoms of Creation and Revelation; in Thy right hand Thou holdest all created things and within Thy grasp are the assigned measures of forgiveness.

Thou forgivest whomsoever among Thy servants Thou pleasest. Verily Thou art the Ever-Forgiving, the All-Loving.

—The Báb

16 Glory be unto Thee, O Lord my God! I beg Thee to forgive me and those who support Thy Faith. Verily Thou art the sovereign Lord, the Forgiver, the Most Generous.

—The Báb

17 The souls who have been enlightened with the light of the Kingdom . . . have found eternal sovereignty. They shine, like unto the stars, upon the horizon of everlasting glory.

—'Abdu'l-Bahá

18 This is eternal sovereignty—to be imbued with the virtues of the human world. This is boundless blessing—to be entirely sanctified and holy above every stain and dross.

—'Abdu'l-Bahá

19 Love is the eternal sovereignty. Love is the divine power.

—'Abdu'l-Bahá

By the Ancient Beauty!—may my life be a sacrifice for His loved ones—Were the friends to realize what a glorious sovereignty the Lord hath destined for them in His Kingdom, surely they would be filled with ecstasy, would behold themselves crowned with immortal glory and carried away with transports of delight.

Erelong it shall be made manifest how brilliantly the light of His bountiful care and mercy hath shone upon His loved ones, and what a turbulent ocean hath been stirred in their hearts! Then will they clamor and exclaim: Happy are we; let all the world rejoice!

—'Abdu'l-Bahá

Dominion

Mulk

Earth and heaven, glory and dominion are God's, the Lord of all men, and the Possessor of the Throne on high and of earth below!
—Bahá'u'lláh

1 Dominion is God's, the Lord of the seen and the unseen, the Lord of creation.

—Bahá'u'lláh

2 O God, my God, and my Desire, and my Adored One, and my Master, and my Mainstay, and my utmost Hope, and my supreme Aspiration! Thou seest me turning towards Thee, holding fast unto the cord of Thy bounty, clinging to the hem of Thy generosity, acknowledging the sanctity of Thy Self and the purity of Thine Essence, and testifying to Thy unity and Thy oneness. I bear witness that Thou art the One, the Single,

the Incomparable, the Ever-Abiding. Thou didst not take unto Thyself a partner in Thy dominion, nor didst Thou choose a peer for Thyself upon earth.

—Bahá'u'lláh

3 No one on earth, O my Lord, can withstand Thy power, and none in all the kingdom of Thy names is able to frustrate Thy purpose. Show forth, then, the power of Thy sovereignty and of Thy dominion, and teach Thy loved ones what beseemeth them in Thy days.

Thou art, verily, the Almighty, the Most Exalted, the All-Glorious, the Most Great.

—Bahá'u'lláh

4 . . . no earthly water can quench the flames of Divine wisdom, nor mortal blasts extinguish the lamp of everlasting dominion.

—Bahá'u'lláh

5 O Son of Man!
Thou art My dominion and My dominion perisheth not; wherefore fearest thou thy perishing? Thou art My light and My light shall never be extinguished; why dost thou dread extinction? Thou art My glory and My glory fadeth not; thou art My robe and My robe shall never be outworn. Abide then in thy love for Me, that thou mayest find Me in the realm of glory.

—Bahá'u'lláh

6 O Son of Being!
    If thine heart be set upon this eternal, imperishable dominion, and this ancient, everlasting life, forsake this mortal and fleeting sovereignty.

—Bahá'u'lláh

7 O My Servant!
    Abandon not for that which perisheth an everlasting dominion, and cast not away celestial sovereignty for a worldly desire. This is the river of everlasting life that hath flowed from the well-spring of the pen of the merciful; well is it with them that drink!

—Bahá'u'lláh

8 Know ye in truth that wealth is a mighty barrier between the seeker and his desire, the lover and his beloved. The rich, but for a few, shall in no wise attain the court of His presence nor enter the city of content and resignation. Well is it then with him, who, being rich, is not hindered by his riches from the eternal kingdom, nor deprived by them of imperishable dominion. By the Most Great Name! The splendor of such a wealthy man shall illuminate the dwellers of heaven even as the sun enlightens the people of the earth!

—Bahá'u'lláh

9 Say: In the East the light of His Revelation hath broken; in the West have appeared the signs of His dominion. . . . Let the Breeze of God awaken you. Verily, it hath wafted over the world. Well is it with him that hath discovered the fragrance thereof and been accounted among the well-assured.

—Bahá'u'lláh

10 Glory to Thee, O my God! . . .
Wert Thou to bestow on one of Thy creatures what would equal the kingdoms of earth and heaven, it would still not diminish by even as much as an atom the immensity of Thy dominion. Far greater art Thou than the Great One men are wont to call Thee, for such a title is but one of Thy names all of which were created by a mere indication of Thy will.

There is no God but Thee, the God of power, the God of glory, the God of knowledge and wisdom.

—Bahá'u'lláh

11 I beg of Thee, O Thou in Whose hands are the kingdoms of earth and heaven, and in Whose grasp lie all who dwell in the dominions of Thy Revelation and Thy creation, not to withhold the glance of Thy favors from such as have sustained tribulations in Thy path . . .

—Bahá'u'lláh

12 All majesty and glory, O my God, and all dominion and light and grandeur and splendor be unto Thee.

—The Báb

May the splendor of what happens to day be Yours!

13 He is God, the Supreme Ruler, the Sovereign Truth, He Whose help is implored by all.

Glorified is He to Whom pertaineth the dominion of the heavens and of the earth, in Whose hand lieth the kingdom of all created things and unto Whom shall all return. It is He Who setteth the measure assigned to each and every thing and revealeth His goodly gifts and blessings in His sacred Book for the benefit of those who offer gratitude for His Cause.

—The Báb

14 O God, my God!

These are servants attracted in Thy days by the fragrances of Thy holiness, enkindled with the flame burning in Thy holy tree, responding to Thy voice, uttering Thy praise, awakened by Thy breeze, stirred by Thy sweet savors, beholding Thy signs, understanding Thy verses, hearkening to Thy words, believing Thy Revelation and assured of Thy loving-kindness. Their eyes, O Lord, are fixed upon Thy kingdom of effulgent glory and their faces turned toward Thy dominion on high, their hearts beating with the love of Thy radiant and glorious beauty, their souls consumed with the flame of Thy love, O Lord of this world and the world hereafter, their lives seething with the ardor of their longing for Thee, and their tears poured forth for Thy sake.

Shield them within the stronghold of Thy protection and safety, preserve them in Thy watchful care, look upon them with the eyes of Thy providence and mercy . . .

—'Abdu'l-Bahá

15 Although men may arise against the Kingdom, the dominion and sovereignty of God will be set up. It is an eternal Kingdom, a divine sovereignty.

—'Abdu'l-Bahá

16 Know thou that all the powers combined have not the power to establish universal peace . . . Erelong, however, shall the power of heaven, the dominion of the Holy Spirit, hoist on the high summits the banners of love and peace, and there above the castles of majesty and might shall those banners wave in the rushing winds that blow out of the tender mercy of God.

—'Abdu'l-Bahá

17 In the estimation of God all men are equal; there is no distinction or preferment for any soul in the dominion of His justice and equity.

—'Abdu'l-Bahá

18 All blessings are divine in origin, but none can be compared with this power of intellectual investigation and research, which is an eternal gift producing fruits of unending delight. Man is ever partaking of these fruits.

All other blessings are temporary; this is an everlasting possession. Even sovereignty has its limitations and overthrow; this is a kingship and dominion which none may usurp or destroy.

Briefly, it is an eternal blessing and divine bestowal, the supreme gift of God to man.

—'Abdu'l-Bahá

19 Rely upon God. Trust in Him. Praise Him, and call Him continually to mind. He verily turneth trouble into ease, and sorrow into solace, and toil into utter peace. He verily hath dominion over all things.

—'Abdu'l-Bahá

Lauded be Thy name, O Lord my God!

I testify that Thou wast a hidden Treasure wrapped within Thine immemorial Being and an impenetrable Mystery enshrined in Thine own Essence. Wishing to reveal Thyself, Thou didst call into being the Greater and the Lesser Worlds, and didst choose Man above all Thy creatures, and didst make Him a sign of both of these worlds, O Thou Who art our Lord, the Most Compassionate!

Thou didst raise Him up to occupy Thy throne before all the people of Thy creation. Thou didst enable Him to unravel Thy mysteries, and to shine with the lights of Thine inspiration and Thy Revelation, and to manifest Thy names and

Thine attributes. Through Him Thou didst adorn the preamble of the book of Thy creation, O Thou Who art the Ruler of the universe Thou hast fashioned!

I bear witness that in His person solidity and fluidity have been joined and combined. Through His immovable constancy in Thy Cause, and His unwavering adherence to whatsoever Thou, in the plenitude of the light of Thy glory, didst unveil to His eyes, throughout the domains of Thy Revelation and creation, the souls of Thy servants were stirred up in their longing for Thy Kingdom, and the dwellers of Thy realms rushed forth to enter into Thy heavenly dominion.

Through the restlessness He evinced in Thy path, the feet of all them that are devoted to Thee were steeled and confirmed to manifest Thy Cause amidst Thy creatures, and to demonstrate Thy sovereignty throughout Thy realm.

How great, O my God, is this Thy most excellent handiwork, and how consummate Thy creation, which hath caused every understanding heart and mind to marvel! And when the set time was fulfilled, and what had been preordained came to pass, Thou didst unloose His tongue to praise Thee, and to lay bare Thy mysteries before all Thy creation, O Thou Who art the Possessor of all names, and the Fashioner of earth and heaven! Through Him all created things were made to glorify Thee, and to celebrate Thy praise, and every soul was directed towards the kingdom of Thy revelation and Thy sovereignty.

—Bahá'u'lláh

Loftiness

'Alá'

Glorified be our Lord, the Most High!
—Bahá'u'lláh

1 Too high art Thou for the praise of those who are nigh unto Thee to ascend unto the heaven of Thy nearness, or for the birds of the hearts of them who are devoted to Thee to attain to the door of Thy gate.

—Bahá'u'lláh

2 Behold, how immeasurably exalted is the Lord your God above all created things.

Witness the majesty of His sovereignty, His ascendancy, and supreme power. If the things which have been created by Him—magnified be His glory—and ordained to be the manifestations of His names and attributes, stand, by virtue of the grace with which they have been endowed, exalted beyond all proximity and remoteness, how much loftier must be that Divine Essence that hath called them into being? . . .

—Bahá'u'lláh

3 By Thy glory! Every time I lift up mine eyes unto Thy heaven, I call to mind Thy highness and Thy loftiness . . .

—Bahá'u'lláh

4 How wondrous is the unity of the Living, the Ever-Abiding God—a unity which is exalted above all limitations, that transcendeth the comprehension of all created things! He hath, from everlasting, dwelt in His inaccessible habitation of holiness and glory, and will unto everlasting continue to be enthroned upon the heights of His independent sovereignty and grandeur.

How lofty hath been His incorruptible Essence, how completely independent of the knowledge of all created things, and how immensely exalted will it remain above the praise of all the inhabitants of the heavens and the earth!

—Bahá'u'lláh

5 How indescribably lofty are the tokens of His consummate power, a single sign of which, however inconsiderable, must transcend the comprehension of

whatsoever hath, from the beginning that hath no beginning, been brought into being, or will be created in the future till the end that hath no end. All the Embodiments of His Names wander in the wilderness of search, athirst and eager to discover His Essence, and all the Manifestations of His Attributes implore Him, from the Sinai of Holiness, to unravel His mystery.

—Bahá'u'lláh

oses "show us your glory."

6 . . . God and His Manifestation can, under no circumstances, be dissociated from the loftiness and sublimity which They inherently possess. Nay, loftiness and sublimity are themselves the creations of His Word, if ye choose to see with My sight not with yours.

—Bahá'u'lláh

7 The whole earth is now in a state of pregnancy. The day is approaching when it will have yielded its noblest fruits, when from it will have sprung forth the loftiest trees, the most enchanting blossoms, the most heavenly blessings.

—Bahá'u'lláh

8 . . . graciously enable Thy servants to recognize what Thou hast ordained for them by Thy bounty and Thy grace. Prescribe for them then through Thy Pen of

Glory that which will direct their steps to the ocean of Thy generosity and will lead them unto the living waters of Thy heavenly reunion.

O Lord! Look not at the things they have wrought, rather look unto the loftiness of Thy celestial bounty which hath preceded all created things, visible and invisible.

O Lord! Illumine their hearts with the effulgent light of Thy knowledge and brighten their eyes with the shining splendor of the day-star of Thy favors.

—Bahá'u'lláh

9 Strive thou day and night to serve the Cause of Him Who is the Eternal Truth, and be thou detached from all else but Him. By Myself! Whatever thou seest in this Day shall perish. Supremely lofty will be thy station, if thou remainest steadfast in the Cause of thy Lord.

—Bahá'u'lláh

10 How lofty is the station which man, if he but choose to fulfill his high destiny, can attain!

—Bahá'u'lláh

march 12

11 The first Taráz [ornament] and the first effulgence which hath dawned from the horizon of the Mother Book is that man should know his own self and

recognize that which leadeth unto loftiness or lowliness, glory or abasement, wealth or poverty.

—Bahá'u'lláh

March 13

12 Lofty is the station of man! Not long ago this exalted Word streamed forth from the treasury of Our Pen of Glory: Great and blessed is this Day—the Day in which all that lay latent in man hath been and will be made manifest. Lofty is the station of man, were he to hold fast to righteousness and truth and to remain firm and steadfast in the Cause. In the eyes of the All-Merciful a true man appeareth even as a firmament; its sun and moon are his sight and hearing, and his shining and resplendent character its stars. His is the loftiest station, and his influence educateth the world of being.

—Bahá'u'lláh

March 14

13 Deign, O my God, I implore Thee, by Thy Self and by them, to accept, through Thy grace and Thy loving-kindness, the works we have performed, however much they fall short of the loftiness of Thy state and the sublimity of Thy station, O Thou Who art most dear to the hearts that long for Thee, and the Healer of the souls that have recognized Thee!

—Bahá'u'lláh

March 15

14 All glory be unto Thee. Immeasurably exalted is that which beseemeth Thee. Verily no one hath ever adequately grasped the loftiness of Thy station, nor hath any one except Thee recognized Thee as beseemeth Thee.

—The Báb

March 16

15 Lauded and glorified art Thou.
 Too exalted is Thy loftiness for the hands of such as are endued with understanding to reach unto Thee, and too profound is Thy fathomless depth for the rivers of men's minds and perceptions to flow out therefrom.

—The Báb

March 17

16 He is exalted above every name, and is sanctified from every comparison. Through Him all things are made known, while too lofty is His reality to be known through anyone but Him.

—The Báb

March 18

17 Men are material; the Manifestations transform them into divine semblance. They are immature children; the Manifestations develop them into maturity. Man is poor; They endow him with wealth. Man is base, treacherous and mean; the Manifestations of God uplift him into dignity, nobility and loftiness.

—'Abdu'l-Bahá

March 19

18 Service to humanity is service to God. Let the love and light of the Kingdom radiate through you until all who look upon you shall be illumined by its reflection. Be as stars, brilliant and sparkling in the loftiness of their heavenly station.

—'Abdu'l-Bahá

March 20

19 Your efforts must be lofty. Exert yourselves with heart and soul so that, perchance, through your efforts the light of universal peace may shine and this darkness of estrangement and enmity may be dispelled from amongst men, that all men may become as one family and consort together in love and kindness, that the East may assist the West and the West give help to the East, for all are the inhabitants of one planet, the people of one original native land and the flocks of one Shepherd.

—'Abdu'l-Bahá

Were man to appreciate the greatness of his station and the loftiness of his destiny he would manifest naught save goodly character, pure deeds, and a seemly and praiseworthy conduct. If the learned and wise men of goodwill were to impart guidance unto the people, the whole earth would be

regarded as one country. Verily this is the undoubted truth. This servant appealeth to every diligent and enterprising soul to exert his utmost endeavor and arise to rehabilitate the conditions in all regions and to quicken the dead with the living waters of wisdom and utterance, by virtue of the love he cherisheth for God, the One, the Peerless, the Almighty, the Beneficent.

—Bahá'u'lláh

PRAYER FOR THE NINETEEN-DAY FEAST

PRAYER FOR THE
NINETEEN-DAY FEAST

. . . keep the Nineteen-Day Feast. It is very important; it is very good. But when you present yourselves in the meetings, before entering them, free yourselves from all that you have in your heart, free your thoughts and your minds from all else save God, and speak to your heart. That all may make this a gathering of love, make it the cause of illumination, make it a gathering of attraction of the hearts, surround this gathering with the Lights of the Supreme Concourse, so that you may be gathered together with the utmost love.

O God!
Dispel all those elements which are the cause of discord, and prepare for us all those things which are the cause of unity and accord!

O God! Descend upon us Heavenly Fragrance and change this gathering into a gathering of Heaven! Grant to us every benefit and every food. Prepare for us the Food of Love! Give to us the Food of Knowledge! Bestow upon us the Food of Heavenly Illumination!

In your hearts remember these things, and then enter the Unity Feast.

—'Abdu'l-Bahá

Notes

Special acknowledgment and thanks are given to Joyce S. Watanabe, who worked tirelessly to help compile, edit, and proofread this book.

Splendor / Bahá

• Bahá'u'lláh, *Gleanings*, p. 29. 1. Ibid., p. 60. 2. Bahá'u'lláh, Kitáb-i Aqdas, ¶42. 3. Ibid., ¶75. 4. Bahá'u'lláh, The Tablet of Carmel, *Tablets of Bahá'u'lláh*, p. 4. 5. Bahá'u'lláh, Kitáb-i Aqdas, ¶111. The first day of the month of Bahá on the Bahá'í calendar is Naw-Rúz, the Bahá'í New Year. 6. Ibid., ¶83. 7. Bahá'u'lláh, from the Kitáb-i 'Ahd, in *Tablets of Bahá'u'lláh*, p. 220. 8. Bahá'u'lláh, quoted in *The Advent of Divine Justice*, p. 76. 9. Bahá'u'lláh, *Prayers and Meditations*, p. 84. 10. Bahá'u'lláh, quoted in *The Advent of Divine Justice*, pp. 75-76. 11. The Báb, *Selections*, pp. 211-12. 12. Ibid., p. 180. 13. 'Abdu'l-Bahá, *Selections*, p. 33. 14. Ibid., p. 5. 15. Ibid., p. 313. 16. Ibid., p. 53. 17. Ibid., p. 314. 18. Ibid., p. 219. 19. Ibid., p. 58. • Ibid., pp. 38-39.

Glory / Jalál

• Bahá'u'lláh, *Gleanings*, p. 96. 1. Bahá'u'lláh, Kitáb-i Aqdas, ¶82. 2. Bahá'u'lláh, *Bahá'í Prayers*, p. 122.3. Bahá'u'lláh, *Prayers and Meditations*, p. 262. 4. Bahá'u'lláh, *Gleanings*, p. 96. 5. Ibid., p. 242. 6. Ibid., p. 308. 7. Bahá'u'lláh, The Hidden Words, Persian, #8. 8. Ibid., #27. 9. Ibid., Arabic, #53. 10. Bahá'u'lláh, *Gleanings*, p. 329. 11. The Báb, *Selections*, p. 186. 12. 'Abdu'l-Bahá, *'Abdu'l-Bahá in London*, p. 20. 13. 'Abdu'l-Bahá, *Paris Talks*, p. 22. 14. 'Abdu'l-Bahá, *The Promulgation of Universal Peace*, p. 180. 15. 'Abdu'l-Bahá, *Selections*, p. 111. 16. Ibid., p. 312. 17. 'Abdu'l-Bahá, *The Promulgation of Universal Peace*, p. 107. 18. 'Abdu'l-Bahá, *Selections*, p. 241. 19. 'Abdu'l-Bahá, *Bahá'í Prayers*, p. 24. • Bahá'u'lláh, *Prayers and Meditations*, pp. 90-94.

Beauty / Jamál

• 'Abdu'l-Bahá, Selections, p. 204. 1. Bahá'u'lláh, The Hidden Words, Arabic, #36. 2. Ibid., Persian, #14. 3. Ibid., #9. 4. Bahá'u'lláh, The Tablet of Ahmad, in Bahá'í Prayers, pp. 209-10. 5. Bahá'u'lláh, Gleanings, p. 283. 6. Bahá'u'lláh, Prayers and Meditations, p. 290. 7. Ibid., p. 261. 8. Ibid., p. 240. 9. Ibid., pp. 178-79. 10 The Báb, Selections, pp. 156-57. 11. Ibid., p. 216. 12. 'Abdu'l-Bahá, Bahá'í Prayers, pp. 32-33. 13. 'Abdu'l-Bahá, Selections, p. 9. 14. Ibid., p. 37. 15. Ibid., p. 6. 16. 'Abdu'l-Bahá, Paris Talks, p. 180. 17. 'Abdu'l-Bahá, Selections, p. 317. 18. Ibid., p. 258. 19. 'Abdu'l-Bahá, 'Abdu'l-Bahá in London, p. 39. • Bahá'u'lláh, Prayers and Meditations, pp. 336-38.

Grandeur / 'Azamat

• Bahá'u'lláh, The Hidden Words, Arabic, #65. 1. Bahá'u'lláh, Prayers and Meditations, p. 295. 2. Ibid., pp. 310-11. 3. Ibid., p. 328. 4. Bahá'u'lláh, 'Ishráqát (Splendors), Tablets of Bahá'u'lláh, p. 114. 5. Bahá'u'lláh, Tablets of Bahá'u'lláh, p. 253. 6. Bahá'u'lláh, The Fire Tablet, Bahá'í Prayers, p. 218. 7. Bahá'u'lláh, Tablet to Fu'ád, Summons of the Lord, p. 177. 8. Bahá'u'lláh, Prayers and Meditations, pp. 170-71. 9. Ibid., p. 173. 10. Bahá'u'lláh, The Hidden Words, Arabic, #65. 11. Bahá'u'lláh, Tablet of the World, Tablets of Bahá'u'lláh, pp. 87-88. 12. The Báb, Selections, p. 217. 13. Ibid., pp. 186-87. 14. Ibid., p. 194. 15. 'Abdu'l-Bahá, Selections, p. 319. 16. Ibid., p. 16. 17. 'Abdu'l-Bahá, Tablet to August Forel, p. 14. 18. 'Abdu'l-Bahá, The Promulgation of Universal Peace, p. 93. 19. 'Abdu'l-Bahá, Selections, p. 4. • 'Abdu'l-Bahá, Bahá'í Prayers, pp. 202-203.

Light / Núr

• Bahá'u'lláh, Epistle to the Son of the Wolf, p. 133. 1. Bahá'u'lláh, Prayers and Meditations, pp. 272-73. 2. Bahá'u'lláh, Gleanings, p. 81. 3. Bahá'u'lláh, Tablets of Bahá'u'lláh, p. 108. 4. Bahá'u'lláh, Prayers and Meditations, p. 12. 5. Bahá'u'lláh, quoted in The Advent of Divine Justice, p. 79. 6. Bahá'u'lláh, Gleanings, pp. 95-96. 7. Bahá'u'lláh, The Hidden Words, Arabic, #33. 8. Ibid., #11. 9. Ibid., #63. 10. Bahá'u'lláh, Kitáb-i Íqán, p. 61. 11. Bahá'u'lláh, Tarázát (Ornaments), Tablets of Bahá'u'lláh, p. 41. 12. The Báb, Selections, p. 61. Cf. Qur'an 5:15-18. 13. 'Abdu'l-Bahá, Tablets of the Divine Plan, p. 65. 14. 'Abdu'l-Bahá, Selections, p. 34. 15. Ibid., pp. 31-32. 16. Ibid., p. 199. 17. 'Abdu'l-Bahá, Secret of Divine Civilization, p. 98. 18. 'Abdu'l-Bahá, Selections, p. 35. 19. The Greatest Holy Leaf, Bahíyyih Khánum, p. 163. • 'Abdu'l-Bahá, Selections, p. 271.

Mercy / Raḥmat

• Bahá'u'lláh, *Gleanings*, p. 286. 1. Bahá'u'lláh, *Prayers and Meditations*, p. 47.
2. Bahá'u'lláh, quoted in *The Advent of Divine Justice*, p. 78. 3. Bahá'u'lláh,
Prayers and Meditations, pp. 24-25. 4. Ibid., pp. 4-5. 5. Ibid., p. 98. 6. Ibid.,
p. 148. 7. Bahá'u'lláh, The Hidden Words, Persian, #29. 8. Ibid., Arabic, #51.
9. Bahá'u'lláh, *Gleanings*, p. 332. 10. Ibid., pp. 99-100. 11. Bahá'u'lláh,
Prayers and Meditations, p. 160. 12. The Báb, *Selections*, p. 163. 13. Ibid.,
p. 183. 14. Ibid., p. 193. 15. Ibid., p. 77. 16. 'Abdu'l-Bahá, *The Promulgation
of Universal Peace*, p. 142. 17. Ibid., p. 150. 18. 'Abdu'l-Bahá, *Paris Talks*,
p. 159. 19. 'Abdu'l-Bahá, *The Promulgation of Universal Peace*, p. 193. • Ibid.,
p. 444.

Words / Kalimát

• Bahá'u'lláh, quoted in *The Advent of Divine Justice*, p.83. 1. Bahá'u'lláh,
Gleanings, p. 183. 2. Ibid., p. 286. 3. Bahá'u'lláh, *Prayers and Meditations*, pp.
295-96. 4. Ibid., p. 113. 5. Bahá'u'lláh, *Epistle to the Son of the Wolf*, p. 4.
6. Bahá'u'lláh, Tablet to Maqsúd, *Tablets of Bahá'u'lláh*, p. 173. 7. Bahá'u'lláh,
The Hidden Words, Persian, #69. 8. Ibid., #76. 9. Ibid., #5. 10. Ibid., #19.
11. Bahá'u'lláh, Tablet of the World, *Tablets of Bahá'u'lláh*, pp. 93-94.
12. Bahá'u'lláh, *Gleanings*, pp. 217-18. 13. Bahá'u'lláh, *Epistle to the Son of the
Wolf*, p. 25. 14. Bahá'u'lláh, *Tablets of Bahá'u'lláh*, p. 172. 15. Bahá'u'lláh,
Tablet to Maqsúd, *Tablets of Bahá'u'lláh*, p. 173. 16. The Báb. *Selections*,
°p. 134. 17. 'Abdu'l-Bahá, *Selections*, p. 73. 18. Ibid., p. 246. 19. Ibid., p. 20.
• Bahá'u'lláh, *Kitáb-i Íqán*, pp. 197-200.

Perfection / Kamál

• The Báb, *Selections*, p. 157. 1. Bahá'u'lláh, *Gleanings*, p. 259. 2. Ibid., p. 62.
3. Bahá'u'lláh, The Hidden Words, Arabic, #12. 4. Ibid., #70. 5. Bahá'u'lláh,
Kitáb-i Íqán, pp. 16-17. 6. Bahá'u'lláh, *Gleanings*, p. 291. 7. 'Abdu'l-Bahá,
Selections, p. 71. 8. 'Abdu'l-Bahá, *Some Answered Questions*, p. 149.
9. 'Abdu'l-Bahá, *Selections*, p. 50. 10 'Abdu'l-Bahá, *Some Answered Questions*,
pp. 235-36. 11. Ibid., p. 235. 12. 'Abdu'l-Bahá, *Paris Talks*, p. 89.
13. 'Abdu'l-Bahá, *Selections*, pp. 128-29. 14. Ibid., p. 69. 15. Ibid., pp. 145-
46. 16. 'Abdu'l-Bahá, *Paris Talks*, p. 16. 17. Ibid., p. 50. 18. 'Abdu'l-Bahá,
Bahá'í Prayers, pp. 31-32. 19. 'Abdu'l-Bahá, *Paris Talks*, p. 114. • 'Abdu'l-
Bahá, *Secret of Divine Civilization*, pp. 35-40.

Names / Aṣmá'

• The Báb, *Selections*, p. 131. 1. Bahá'u'lláh, *Prayers and Meditations*, p. 31.
2. Bahá'u'lláh, Kitáb-i Aqdas, ¶78. 3. Bahá'u'lláh, *Gleanings*, p. 310. 4. Ibid.,
p. 204. 5. Bahá'u'lláh, *Prayers and Meditations*, p. 23. 6. Ibid., pp. 21-22.

7. Bahá'u'lláh, Kitáb-i Aqdas, ¶132. 8. Bahá'u'lláh, *Prayers and Meditations*, p. 118. 9. Bahá'u'lláh, *Gleanings*, p. 203. 10 . Ibid., p. 177. 11. Ibid., p. 65. 12. Bahá'u'lláh, *Prayers and Meditations*, p. 21. 13. The Báb, *Selections*, p. 125. 14. 'Abdu'l-Bahá, *The Promulgation of Universal Peace*, p. 422. 15. Ibid., pp. 158-59. 16. Ibid., p. 219. 17. 'Abdu'l-Bahá, *Some Answered Questions*, p. 196. 18. Ibid., p. 9. Cf. Gen. 1:26. 19. 'Abdu'l-Bahá, *Selections*, p. 41. • Bahá'u'lláh, *Prayers and Meditations*, pp. 219-20.

Might / 'Izzat

• Bahá'u'lláh, *Gleanings*, p. 242. 1. Bahá'u'lláh, *Epistle to the Son of the Wolf*, p. 105. 2. Bahá'u'lláh, Tablet of the Proof, *Tablets of Bahá'u'lláh*, p. 210. 3. Bahá'u'lláh, *Summons of the Lord*, p. 39.   4. Bahá'u'lláh, *Prayers and Meditations*, pp. 46-47. 5. Bahá'u'lláh, *Gleanings*, pp. 16-17. 6. Bahá'u'lláh, *Epistle to the Son of the Wolf*, p. 151. 7. Bahá'u'lláh, *Prayers and Meditations*, p. 197. 8. Bahá'u'lláh, *Bahá'í Prayers*, p. 92. 9. Bahá'u'lláh, *Tablets of Bahá'u'lláh*, p. 233. 10. Bahá'u'lláh, *Prayers and Meditations*, p. 264. 11. The Báb, *Selections*, p. 4. 12. Ibid., pp. 166-67. 13. 'Abdu'l-Bahá, *The Promulgation of Universal Peace*, p. 82. 14. 'Abdu'l-Bahá,. *Selections*, p. 5. 15. 'Abdu'l-Bahá, *The Promulgation of Universal Peace*, p. 302. 16. 'Abdu'l-Bahá, *Tablets of the Divine Plan*, p. 107. 17. 'Abdu'l-Bahá. *Selections*, p. 313. 18. 'Abdu'l-Bahá, *Paris Talks*, p. 107. 19. 'Abdu'l-Bahá, *The Promulgation of Universal Peace*, p. 20.   • Bahá'u'lláh, quoted in *God Passes By*, p. x.

Will / Mashíyyat

• The Báb, *Selections*, p. 210. 1. Bahá'u'lláh, *Prayers and Meditations*, p. 90. 2. Bahá'u'lláh, *Gleanings*, p. 141. 3. Bahá'u'lláh, Words of Paradise, *Tablets of Bahá'u'lláh*, p. 67. 4. Ibid., p. 59. 5. Bahá'u'lláh, *Prayers and Meditations*, p. 68. 6. Ibid., p. 11. 7. Ibid., p. 193. 8. Bahá'u'lláh, *Gleanings*, p. 311. 9. Bahá'u'lláh, *Prayers and Meditations*, p. 240. 10. Bahá'u'lláh, *Gleanings*, p. 343. 11. Bahá'u'lláh, 'Ishráqát (Splendors), *Tablets of Bahá'u'lláh*, pp. 109-110. 12. Bahá'u'lláh, *Prayers and Meditations*, p. 55. 13. Bahá'u'lláh, *Gleanings*, p. 197. 14. The Báb, *Selections*, p. 198. 15. Ibid., p. 214. 16. 'Abdu'l-Bahá, *'Abdu'l-Bahá in London*, pp. 19-20. 17. 'Abdu'l-Bahá, *Selections*, p. 26. 18. 'Abdu'l-Bahá, *Paris Talks*, p. 54. 19. The Greatest Holy Leaf, *Bahíyyih Khánum*, p. 97. • Bahá'u'lláh, *Gleanings*, pp. 337-38.

Knowledge / 'Ilm

• Bahá'u'lláh, *Gleanings*, p. 5. 1. Bahá'u'lláh, 'Ishráqát (Splendors), *Tablets of Bahá'u'lláh*, p. 103. 2. Bahá'u'lláh, *Epistle to the Son of the Wolf*, p. 98. 3. Bahá'u'lláh, *Prayers and Meditations*, p. 213. 4. Bahá'u'lláh, The Tablet of the Virgin, *Spiritual Strength for Men*, p. 158. 5. Bahá'u'lláh, *Kitáb-i Íqán*,

pp. 99-100.   6. Bahá'u'lláh, *Prayers and Meditations*, p. 177.   7. Ibid., p. 38.
8. Bahá'u'lláh, "Tablet of the True Seeker," *Kitáb-i Íqán*, p. 3.   9. Ibid., pp. 3-
4.   10. Bahá'u'lláh, Tajallíyát (Effulgences), *Tablets of Bahá'u'lláh*, pp. 51-52.
11. Ibid., Tablet of the Proof, pp. 207-208.   12. Bahá'u'lláh, *Kitáb-i Íqán*,
p. 211.   13. Bahá'u'lláh, *Gleanings*, p. 312.   14. Ibid., p. 160.   15. 'Abdu'l-Bahá,
The Promulgation of Universal Peace, p. 228.   16. 'Abdu'l-Bahá, *Bahá'í Prayers*,
p. 103.   17. 'Abdu'l-Bahá, *The Promulgation of Universal Peace*, p. 249.
18. 'Abdu'l-Bahá, *Selections*, p. 221.   19. Ibid., p. 266.   • Bahá'u'lláh, The
Seven Valleys, from The Valley of Knowledge.

Power / Qudrat

• Bahá'u'lláh, *Prayers and Meditations*, p. 326.   1. Ibid., p. 211.   2. Bahá'u'lláh,
Prayers and Meditations, p. 60.   3. Bahá'u'lláh, *Kitáb-i Íqán*, p. 176.
4. Bahá'u'lláh, *Prayers and Meditations*, pp. 176-77.   5. Ibid., p. 275.   6. Ibid.,
pp. 164-65.   7. Bahá'u'lláh, *Gleanings*, p. 300.   8. Bahá'u'lláh, The Hidden
Words, Arabic, #34   9. Ibid., #13.   10. Bahá'u'lláh, *Prayers and Meditations*,
p. 174.   11. Ibid., p. 256.   12. Bahá'u'lláh, *Gleanings*, p. 287.   13. The Báb,
Selections, p. 198.   14. Ibid., p. 213.   15. Ibid., p. 153.   16. 'Abdu'l-Bahá,
Selections, pp. 260-61.   17. Ibid., p. 104.   18. Ibid., p. 310.   19. 'Abdu'l-Bahá,
Tablets of the Divine Plan, p. 81.   • 'Abdu'l-Bahá, *Selections*, p. 27.

Speech / Qawl

• Bahá'u'lláh, quoted in *The Advent of Divine Justice*, p. 82.   1. Bahá'u'lláh,
'Ishráqát (Splendors), *Tablets of Bahá'u'lláh*, p. 101.   2. Ibid., Words of
Paradise, p. 57.   3. Ibid., 'Ishráqát (Splendors), p. 101.   4. Bahá'u'lláh, *Prayers
and Meditations*, p. 283.   5. Ibid., p. 114.   6. Ibid., p. 269.   7. Bahá'u'lláh, The
Hidden Words, Persian, #16.   8. Bahá'u'lláh, Tablet to Sayyid Mihdí Dahají,
Tablets of Bahá'u'lláh, pp. 197-98.   9. Bahá'u'lláh, *Gleanings*, p. 285.
10. Bahá'u'lláh, Kitáb-i 'Ahd (The Book of the Covenant), *Tablets of
Bahá'u'lláh*, pp. 219-20.   11. Bahá'u'lláh, *Gleanings*, p. 304.   12. Bahá'u'lláh,
Tablet to Sayyid Mihdí Dahají, *Tablets of Bahá'u'lláh*, p. 200.   13. 'Abdu'l-
Bahá, *'Abdu'l-Bahá in London*, pp. 126-27.   14. 'Abdu'l-Bahá, *Selections*, p. 30.
15. Ibid., p. 268.   16. Ibid., pp. 268-69.   17. 'Abdu'l-Bahá, *The Promulgation of
Universal Peace*, p. 390.   18. Ibid., p. 197.   19. 'Abdu'l-Bahá, *Selections*, p. 93.
• Bahá'u'lláh, Tablet to Maqsúd, *Tablets of Bahá'u'lláh*, pp. 172-73.

Questions / Masá'il

• Imám 'Alí, quoted by Bahá'u'lláh in The Seven Valleys, p. 34.   See also,
'Abdu'l-Bahá, *Secret of Divine Civilization*, p. 19.   1. Bahá'u'lláh, Kitáb-i Aqdas,
¶55.   2. Bahá'u'lláh, *Prayers and Meditations*, p. 195.   3. Bahá'u'lláh, The
Hidden Words, Persian, #4.   4. Bahá'u'lláh, *Epistle to the Son of the Wolf*, p. 95.

5. Bahá'u'lláh, *Prayers and Meditations*, p. 83. 6. Bahá'u'lláh, Kitáb-i Aqdas, ¶126. 7. Bahá'u'lláh, Tablet to Vafá, *Tablets of Bahá'u'lláh*, p. 183. 8. Baha'u'llah, *Kitáb-i Íqán*, pp. 8-9, quoting Qur'an 29:2. 9. Bahá'u'lláh, *Gems of Divine Mysteries*, p. 13. 10. Bahá'u'lláh, *Gleanings*, pp. 93-94. 11. The Báb, *Selections*, p. 217. 12. Ibid., p. 153. 13. 'Abdu'l-Bahá, *The Wisdom of the Master*, p. 96. 14. 'Abdu'l-Bahá, *The Promulgation of Universal Peace*, p. 8. 15. 'Abdu'l-Bahá, *The Wisdom of the Master*, p. 97. 16. 'Abdu'l-Bahá, *The Promulgation of Universal Peace*, p. 213. 17. 'Abdu'l-Bahá, *Secret of Divine Civilization*, p. 103. 18. 'Abdu'l-Bahá, *The Promulgation of Universal Peace*, p. 190. 19. Ibid., p. 52. • Bahá'u'lláh, *Bahá'í Prayers*, pp. 214-20.

Honor / Sharaf

• 'Abdu'l-Bahá, *The Promulgation of Universal Peace*, p. 166. 1. Bahá'u'lláh, *Prayers and Meditations*, p. 335. 2. Bahá'u'lláh, *Gleanings*, p. 64. 3. Bahá'u'lláh, *Prayers and Meditations*, pp. 94-95. 4. Bahá'u'lláh, *Gleanings*, p. 334. 5. Ibid., p. 306. 6. Ibid., pp. 9-10. 7. Ibid., pp. 86-87. 8. Ibid., pp. 305-306. 9. The Báb, *Bahá'í Prayers*, p. 151. 10. 'Abdu'l-Bahá, *The Promulgation of Universal Peace*, p. 166. 11. Ibid., p. 335. 12. 'Abdu'l-Bahá, *Some Answered Questions*, pp. 79-80. 13. Ibid., p. 137. 14. 'Abdu'l-Bahá, *Secret of Divine Civilization*, p. 71. 15. Ibid., p. 19. 16. 'Abdu'l-Bahá, *The Promulgation of Universal Peace*, p. 332. 17. Ibid., p. 348. 18. Ibid., p. 361. 19. Ibid., p. 397. • 'Abdu'l-Bahá, *Foundations of World Unity*, pp. 42-43.

Sovereignty / Sultán

• Bahá'u'lláh, *Gleanings*, p. 42. 1. Bahá'u'lláh, *Prayers and Meditations*, p. 3. 2. Bahá'u'lláh, *Gleanings*, p. 302. 3. Bahá'u'lláh, *Epistle to the Son of the Wolf*, p. 24. 4. Bahá'u'lláh, *Gleanings*, pp. 29-30. 5. Bahá'u'lláh, *Prayers and Meditations*, p. 248. 6. Bahá'u'lláh, *Gleanings*, p. 184. 7. Ibid., p. 73. 8. Baha'u'llah, *Kitáb-i Íqán*, pp. 107-108. 9. Bahá'u'lláh, *Epistle to the Son of the Wolf*, p. 95. 10. Bahá'u'lláh. *The Hidden Words*, Arabic, #1. 11. Ibid., #15. 12. Ibid., Persian, #41. 13. Bahá'u'lláh, *Tablets of Bahá'u'lláh*, p. 247. 14. Ibid., p. 266. 15. The Báb, *Selections*, p. 178. 16. Ibid., p. 200. 17. 'Abdu'l-Bahá, *Bahá'í World Faith*, p. 166. 18. 'Abdu'l-Bahá, *The Promulgation of Universal Peace*, p. 186. 19. Ibid., p. 211. • 'Abdu'l-Bahá, *Selections*, p. 309.

Dominion / Mulk

• Bahá'u'lláh, *Prayers and Meditations*, Medium Obligatory Prayer, p. 315. 1. Bahá'u'lláh, Kitáb-i Aqdas, ¶11. Prayer to be said on the appearance of fearful natural events. 2. Bahá'u'lláh, *Epistle to the Son of the Wolf*, p. 3. 3. Bahá'u'lláh, Ibid., p. 16. 4. Bahá'u'lláh, *Gleanings*, p. 19. 5. Bahá'u'lláh,

The Hidden Words, Arabic, #14. 6. Ibid., #54. 7. Ibid., Persian, #37. 8. Ibid., #53. 9. Bahá'u'lláh, The Most Holy Tablet, *Tablets of Bahá'u'lláh*, p. 13. 10. Bahá'u'lláh, *Prayers and Meditations*, pp. 156-57. 11. Ibid., pp. 286-87. 12. The Báb, *Selections*, p. 202. 13. Ibid., pp. 160-61. 14. 'Abdu'l-Bahá, *Bahá'í Prayers*, pp. 156-57. 15. 'Abdu'l-Bahá, *The Promulgation of Universal Peace*, p. 212. 16. 'Abdu'l-Bahá, *Selections*, p. 174. 17. 'Abdu'l-Bahá, *The Promulgation of Universal Peace*, p. 182. 18. Ibid., p. 50. 19. 'Abdu'l-Bahá, *Selections*, p. 178. • Bahá'u'lláh, *Prayers and Meditations*, pp. 48-50.

Loftiness / 'Alá'

• Bahá'u'lláh, Tablet of the Holy Mariner. 1. Bahá'u'lláh, *Prayers and Meditations*, p. 320. 2. Bahá'u'lláh, *Gleanings*, pp. 184-85. 3. Bahá'u'lláh, *Prayers and Meditations*, p. 272. 4. Bahá'u'lláh, *Gleanings*, pp. 261-62. 5. Ibid., p. 61. 6. Ibid., p. 73. 7. Bahá'u'lláh, quoted in *The Promised Day Is Come*, p. 117. 8. Bahá'u'lláh, Tablet to Maqsúd, *Tablets of Bahá'u'lláh*, pp. 177-78. 9. Bahá'u'lláh, *Gleanings*, p. 246. 10. Ibid., p. 206. 11. Bahá'u'lláh, Tarázát (Ornaments), *Tablets of Bahá'u'lláh*, pp. 34-35. 12. Ibid., p. 220. 13. Bahá'u'lláh, *Prayers and Meditations*, p. 299. 14. The Báb, *Selections*, p. 195. 15. Ibid., p. 195. 16. Ibid., p. 125. 17. 'Abdu'l-Bahá, *The Promulgation of Universal Peace*, p. 466. 18. Ibid., p. 8. 19. Ibid., p. 469. • Bahá'u'lláh, Tablet to Maqsúd, *Tablets of Bahá'u'lláh*, p. 172.

BIBLIOGRAPHY

'Abdu'l-Bahá, *'Abdu'l-Bahá in London* (London: Bahá'í Publishing Trust, 1921 [1982]).

_____, *Bahá'í World Faith: Selected Writings of Bahá'u'lláh and 'Abdu'l-Bahá* (Wilmette, Ill.: Bahá'í Publishing Trust, 1956).

_____, *Foundations of World Unity* (Wilmette, Ill.: Bahá'í Publishing Trust, 1945).

_____, *Paris Talks: Addresses Given by 'Abdu'l-Bahá in Paris* (London: Bahá'í Publishing Trust, 1912 [1972]).

_____, *The Promulgation of Universal Peace: Talks delivered by 'Abdu'l-Bahá during His Visit to the United States and Canada in 1912*. Revised Edition. Comp. by Howard MacNutt (Wilmette, Ill.: Bahá'í Publishing Trust, 1912 [1982]).

_____, *The Secret of Divine Civilization* (Wilmette, Ill.: Bahá'í Publishing Trust, 1957).

_____, *Selections from the Writings of 'Abdu'l-Bahá* (Haifa: Bahá'í World Center, 1978).

_____, *Some Answered Questions* (Wilmette, Ill.: Bahá'í Publishing Trust, 1908 [1981]).

_____, *Tablet to August Forel*, in various compilations, see for example, *The Bahá'í World*, Vol. 15, 1968-1973 (Haifa: Bahá'í World Center, 1976) pp. 37-43.

_____, *The Tablets of the Divine Plan* (Wilmette, Ill.: Bahá'í Publishing Trust, 1959 [1977]).

The Báb, *Selections from the Writings of the Báb* (Haifa: Bahá'í World Center, 1976).

Bahá'u'lláh, *Epistle to the Son of the Wolf* (Wilmette, Ill.: Bahá'í Publishing Trust, 1941).

_____, *The Gems of Divine Mysteries* (Haifa: Bahá'í World Center, 2002).

_____, *Gleanings from the Writings of Bahá'u'lláh* (Wilmette, Ill.: Bahá'í Publishing Trust, 1939).

_____, The Hidden Words (various publishers and editions).

_____, The Kitáb-i Aqdas (various publishers and editions).

_____, *The Kitáb-i Íqán* (Wilmette, Ill.: Bahá'í Publishing Trust, 1931).

_____, *Prayers and Meditations by Bahá'u'lláh* (Wilmette, Ill.: Bahá'í Publishing Trust, 1938).

_____, The Seven Valleys (various publishers and editions).

_____, *The Summons of the Lord of Hosts* (Haifa: Bahá'í World Center, 2002).

_____, Tablet of the Holy Mariner, in various compilations, see for example, Michael Sours, *The Tablet of the Holy Mariner: An Illustrated Guide to Bahá'u'lláh's Mystical Writing in the Sufi Tradition* (Los Angeles: Kalimát Press, 2002).

_____, *Tablets of Bahá'u'lláh revealed after the Kitáb-i-Aqdas* (Haifa: Bahá'í World Center, 1978 [1988]).

Bahá'í Prayers: A Selection of Prayers Revealed by Bahá'u'lláh, the Báb, and 'Abdu'l-Bahá (Wilmette, Ill.: Bahá'í Publishing Trust, 1954 [1991]).

Bahíyyih Khánum, *Bahíyyih Khánum, The Greatest Holy Leaf* (Haifa: Bahá'í World Center, 1982).

Shoghi Effendi, *The Advent of Divine Justice* (Wilmette, Ill.: Bahá'í Publishing Trust, 1939).

_____, *God Passes By* (Wilmette, Ill.: Bahá'í Publishing Trust, 1944).

_____, *The Promised Day Is Come*, (Wilmette, Ill.: Bahá'í Publishing Trust, 1941).

Spiritual Strength for Men: Selections from the Writings of Bahá'u'lláh, the Báb, and 'Abdu'l-Bahá (Los Angeles: Kalimát Press, 2003).

The Wisdom of the Master: The Spiritual Teachings of 'Abdu'l-Bahá (Los Angeles: Kalimát Press, 1997).